Celebrating Ch
Learning

In response to growing pressure on early years practitioners to adopt a 'tick-box' approach to recording children's progress, *Celebrating Children's Learning* sets out a bold, alternative vision for assessment in the early years. Drawing upon an inspiring collaboration between London nursery schools, this book explores and reconsiders the purpose of observation in early years settings.

Contributors provide a range of examples to guide early years practitioners as they develop their own methods of observation. Play, social interaction, and cooperation with parents are shown to be valuable opportunities for keen observation. Chapters discuss:

- moving beyond data-focussed assessment
- Characteristics of Effective Learning
- ensuring inclusive assessment
- collaborating with parents from diverse backgrounds
- outdoor learning – a Forest School approach.

Inspiring and empowering, *Celebrating Children's Learning* is essential reading for teachers, practitioners and students involved in early education.

Julian Grenier is the headteacher of Sheringham Nursery School and Children's Centre in East London, UK, and is a National Leader of Education.

Sue Finch has worked in the early years sector for over 40 years and is a highly experienced education consultant. Sue has worked on a wide range of national projects in the early years, including the Pen Green Teaching Centres Project.

Caroline Vollans worked as a primary school teacher for 15 years before completing clinical training in Lacanian psychoanalysis. She now works as a student counsellor, as well as providing staff supervision in nursery settings.

Celebrating Children's Learning

*Assessment Beyond Levels
in the Early Years*

Edited by
Julian Grenier, Sue Finch and
Caroline Vollans

National Teaching School
designated by

National College for
Teaching & Leadership

Routledge
Taylor & Francis Group

LONDON AND NEW YORK

First published 2018
by Routledge
2 Park Square, Milton Park, Abingdon, Oxon OX14 4RN

and by Routledge
711 Third Avenue, New York, NY 10017

Routledge is an imprint of the Taylor & Francis Group, an informa business

British Library Cataloguing-in-Publication Data
A catalogue record for this book is available from the British Library

Library of Congress Cataloging-in-Publication Data
Names: Grenier, Julian, editor.
Title: Celebrating children's learning : assessment beyond levels in the early
    years / [edited by Julian Grenier, Sue Finch, Caroline Vollans].
Description: Abingdon, Oxon ; New York, NY : Routledge, 2017. |
    Includes bibliographical references.
Identifiers: LCCN 2017037297 (print) | LCCN 2017053935 (ebook) |
    ISBN 9781315149400 (ebook) | ISBN 9781138555259 (hardback) |
    ISBN 9781138555273 (pbk.) | ISBN 9781315149400 (ebk)
Subjects: LCSH: Early childhood education—England—London—
    Evaluation. | Observation (Educational method)Classification: LCC
    LB1139.3.G7 (ebook) | LCC LB1139.3.G7 C45 2017 (print) | DDC
    372.21094212—dc23
LC record available at https://lccn.loc.gov/2017037297

ISBN: 978-1-138-55525-9 (hbk)
ISBN: 978-1-138-55527-3 (pbk)
ISBN: 978-1-315-14940-0 (ebk)

Typeset in Optima
by Apex CoVantage, LLC

Contents

Foreword

In my role leading the Chartered College of Teaching, I seek to connect teachers to become recognized, informed and inspired. Expertise and sharing of knowledge about how best to provide an excellent learning experience for all children must start with the adults in every setting, school and college. I am very pleased, therefore, to provide a preface for this important book.

Within these pages, you will find rich stories of children's development, play and learning that offer profound glimpses and insights. Colleagues leading this project have realized that tracking is not assessment and learning is not linear. Data sheets, endless post-its and tick-boxes cannot hope to achieve what a professional educator can assimilate through close observation, detailed listening and empathic engagement. The education offered to our youngest children forms the building blocks for all that is to come. When we create magic in the early years, our children thrive.

Practitioners in these nursery schools offer expertise in assessment that truly starts with the child and puts learning first. I love the way that this project successfully puts assessment where it needs to be, as a means of building deep insightful understanding of children. The rest of our education system would do well to remember this premise and to act upon it.

Professor Dame Alison Peacock

Acknowledgements

We would like to thank the following people, schools and organisations for contributing observations and assessments, and helping to select materials:

Claire Barber and Gill Crowley, Abbey Wood Nursery School – Greenwich

Sandra Campbell, Church Hill and Low Hall Nursery Schools Federation – Waltham Forest

Adam Lane, Clyde Nursery School – Lewisham

Jo Aylett, Edith Kerrison Nursery School – Newham

Kelly Hall, Kaizen Primary School – Newham

Sarah Porter, Kay Rowe Nursery School – Newham

Stella Wybron, Oliver Thomas Nursery School – Newham

Teresa Lane, Rachel McMillan Nursery School – Greenwich

Sarah Davies, Robert Owen Nursery School – Greenwich

Karla Davis, Ronald Openshaw Nursery Education Centre – Newham

Julian Grenier and Lesley Webb, Sheringham Nursery School – Newham

Linda Mullis, Governor, Sheringham Nursery School – Newham

Peter Catling and Jenny Baker, Woodlands Park Nursery School – Haringey

Nicola Blatchly-Lewis, Strategic Manager of Newham's Early Years Learning and Achievement Team

East London Early Years and Schools Partnership Teaching School Alliance (ELEYSP) (www.eleysp.co.uk)

South Thames Early Education Partnership and Teaching School Alliance (STEEP) (www.steeptsa.org.uk)

Sue Finch, early years consultant

Helen Moylett, early years consultant

Nancy Stewart, early years consultant

Editor and contributor biographies

Tania Choudhury

Tania was born and raised in East London where her parents had migrated to from Bangladesh in the early 80s. After graduating in history, her passion for making a difference to young people's lives was nurtured by the Teach First programme, which led to her teaching career in early education. She teaches at Sheringham nursery school in Newham, East London, and is an accredited Special Educational Needs Co-ordinator (SENCO). Tania has mastered four languages, all of which she uses when interacting with parents. She is passionate about working closely with parents to ensure high quality engagement, particularly those who may be regarded as finding services hard to reach, and collaborates with the children's centre to ensure vulnerable families are well supported. Tania organises events at the nursery school and children's centre to celebrate and encourage the diversity and vibrancy of the local community.

Sue Finch

Sue facilitated the Celebrating Children's Learning group meetings that led to this book, and has helped to organise the Learning Without Limits network in Newham for the last three years. She worked on the Early Years Teaching Centres programme led by Pen Green Research Centre, and mentors a nursery school headteacher who manages the early years advisory teachers in her borough. Sue has worked in the early years sector for over 40 years. Her career in early education began with developing a community nursery in the London Borough of Hackney, then opening and managing a nursery and children's centre for the same borough. Sue also worked for the Department for Education (DfE) as an adviser during the development of the children's centre programme.

Julian Grenier

Julian is the headteacher of Sheringham Nursery School and Children's Centre in Newham, East London, and is a National Leader of Education. He has a doctorate in education from the Institute of Education. Julian was a member of the Expert Advisory Panel for the Nutbrown Review of Early Years Qualifications and the Rose Review of the Primary Curriculum. He is the former National Chair of Early Education.

Sheringham Nursery School co-leads the East London Partnership, the Teaching School Alliance that developed Celebrating Children's Learning.

Julian is the author of *Successful Early Years Ofsted Inspections* (Sage, 2016). He is an occasional blogger and tweets @juliangrenier.

Alison Lentz

Alison is the head teacher of Ronald Openshaw Nursery, an inclusive nursery school in Newham. In addition, she manages the SEND Hub for early years, supporting all private, voluntary and independent settings across the borough. Furthermore, she is currently leading the 'early years and early identification' strand of Newham's new Best For All inclusion strategy. She is committed to professionals learning in partnership with parents, support services and other settings.

Helen Moylett

Helen is an independent early years trainer, consultant and writer. She has been head teacher of an early years centre as well as working in schools and as a primary and early years lecturer at Manchester Metropolitan University. While working for the National Strategies, she was centrally involved in developing the Early Years Foundation Stage and was the national lead for the Every Child a Talker (ECAT) programme. She co-authored *Development Matters* with Nancy Stewart and has written and edited several early years books – most recently, *Characteristics of Effective Early Learning: Helping Young Children Become Learners for Life* (OU Press 2014). Helen is currently a Vice-President of Early Education and a tutor on the PGCE and MA courses at the Centre for Research in Early Childhood in Birmingham.

Megan Panayiotou

Megan is an experienced teacher and Special Educational Needs Co-ordinator (SENCO) in Ronald Openshaw inclusive nursery school. As well as co-ordinating support for all the children with additional needs, Megan manages the resource provision for children with profound and multiple learning difficulties, providing intensive support to meet their many and varied needs. Megan has introduced a menu of small group interactions for targeted children and ensures that these are inclusive for the maximum benefit of all learners.

Nancy Stewart

Nancy is a consultant and writer with wide experience across early years sectors in schools, nurseries, local authority advisory service and the National Strategies, where she was Senior Early Years Adviser with a central role in ECAT. She also served as lecturer and assessor for Early Years Professional Status with Edge Hill and Manchester Metropolitan Universities. Nancy provided expert advice to the review of the Early Years Foundation Stage, drawing on her interest in children's development as self-regulating learners. Her writing includes *How Children Learn: The Characteristics of Effective Early Learning* (Early Education 2012) and she co-authored *Development Matters in the EYFS* with Helen Moylett. Nancy currently serves as Vice Chair of TACTYC, the Association for Professional Development in the Early Years.

Caroline Vollans

Caroline worked as a primary school teacher for 15 years before doing an MA and clinical training in psychoanalysis. She now works as a counsellor in a secondary school and is a regular feature writer for *Nursery World*. Caroline is the author of *Wise Words: How Susan Isaacs Changed Parenting* (Routledge, 2017)

Lesley Webb

Lesley has been a teacher for over 30 years; most of that time has been spent with nursery and reception children. After several years teaching in London, she became an Early Years Advisor in the London Borough of Newham. During eight years in this post, she had responsibility, within the team, for ECAT and children under three. She also worked with Early Education on the Newham Outdoors project. Lesley was then seconded four days a week to acting deputy head at a nursery school, before taking on the substantive post full time. She went on to be Deputy Head at Sheringham Nursery School and Children's Centre where she has continued to develop her interests in communication, language and the outdoors. Two years ago, Lesley obtained the Level 3 Forest School leaders qualification and has since led Forest School at Sheringham Nursery School.

Introduction
Sue Finch

Many early years practitioners and students report that they are struggling with the burden of assessment, finding it too time-consuming; this book aims to answer their cry for help.

Practitioners endlessly scribble on post-it notes or hold up iPads to snap photos of children so that they can collect evidence of their learning, when those children would do better if they had someone to listen to them, play with them and help them to think critically. In this age of measurement and ranking, we are in danger of placing so much emphasis on learning journeys, online journals and collections of assessment information that we end up neglecting what matters: children's minute-by-minute experiences in the early years, and our opportunities to support their learning, offer them the best possible care, and teach them new skills.

Concerned about this growing tendency for children's progress merely to be recorded by using tick-lists and complicated tracking systems, a group of London nursery schools met in early 2016 to share their ways of celebrating children's play, development and learning. The schools were brought together by Julian Grenier, Headteacher of Sheringham Nursery School in Newham, the lead school in the East London Early Years and Schools Partnership Teaching School Alliance. All were concerned that most practitioners across the early years sector were spending too much time on assessment that simply ticked off – or repeated – the 461 statements in *Development Matters* (2012) and the *Early Years Outcomes* (2013) about the progress of children under five, leaving too little time for playing and interacting with children, encouraging creativity and critical thinking, and promoting the 'whole child' as a competent and creative learner.

The *Development Matters* (DfE, 2012) guidance to the statutory frame-work for the Early Years Foundation Stage (EYFS) was never intended to be used like this; every page states that 'Children develop at their own rates, and in their own ways. The development statements and their order should not be taken as necessary steps for individual children. They should not be used as checklists'. Yet a whole range of check-lists and software has sprung up to point practitioners in the opposite direction, and many settings buy into assessment schemes that are marketed as helping them to comply with Ofsted inspection requirements by 'ticking off' the *Development Matters* statements for each child at every stage of their development.

Ofsted makes it clear, however, that inspectors are not looking for a par-ticular form of assessment:

> There is no prescribed way of conducting or recording assessments, as long as it is effective and helps children's learning, development and progress.
>
> (online guidance to *Early Years Inspection*: *Myths*, 2017b)

The Ofsted early years inspection handbook (2015b, p. 36) is equally clear that when assessing the quality of teaching, learning and assessment in a setting:

> The main evidence comes from the inspectors' direct observations of the way in which children demonstrate the key Characteristics of Effective Learning:
>
> * Playing and exploring
> * Active learning
> * Creating and thinking critically
>
> and their evaluation of how practitioners' teaching supports the learn-ing of children of different ages.
>
> (Ofsted, 2015b, p. 36)

The 12 London nursery schools decided to create a free online resource of observations and assessments that would celebrate children's exploration, active learning and thinking as well as inclusion, learning outdoors, par-ent involvement, and the freedom of girls and boys to play and learn out-side of rigid gender roles. We recognised that some of the best learning is cross-curricular, but agreed to share observations and assessments under the headings used in *Development Matters* (Characteristics of Effective Learning, Areas and Aspects of Learning) to keep the resources accessible, readable and connected to the EYFS framework for practitioners. Through consideration of examples, we proposed that rich detail (in writing and/or photos) prompts reflection, dialogue, and focussed discussions that support moderation. At the same time, we wanted to see a reduction in assessment quantity and bureaucracy, and more emphasis on dialogue about learning and thinking about next steps (further explored by Julian Grenier in Chapter 1, 'Beyond data').

The nursery schools agreed that there was no single approach, format, style or tone of observation that is 'correct'. Our hope was that a range of high-quality examples would support practitioners in choosing and developing an approach that suited their particular context. Each of the nursery schools collected and shared observations and assessments of children that exemplified the Characteristics of Effective Learning, and particular areas and aspects of learning, across different age/stage bands. For example:

> Eshan spent a long time cutting several pieces of string with the help of Sandra (the practitioner). Eshan counted how many pieces he had and Sandra found a little box for him to keep them in. Eshan cut some more pieces of string, counting as he went. He wanted to keep cutting more and more pieces because he enjoyed cutting, sticking, and counting beyond the number he had reached. He counted all that way up to 30. Sandra then helped him to find some paper for him to stick each piece of string down.
>
> (Exemplifies Mathematics: Numbers 40–60+ months, see East London Early Years and Schools Partnership, 2017, www.eleysp. co.uk/celebrating-childrens-learning/Mathematics-Numbers)

The nursery schools working on Celebrating Children's Learning were joined by early years consultants Helen Moylett and Nancy Stewart, who had written the initial *Development Matters* guidance (Early Education, 2012), and they selected the observations that best exemplified the Characteristics of Effective Learning (see their Chapter 2, 'Putting the Characteristics of Effective Learning at the heart of assessment'). A panel that included Helen and Nancy, Linda Mullis (Chair of Governors at Sheringham Nursery School) and Nicola Blatchly-Lewis (Strategic Manager for Learning and Achievement in Newham) moderated the final selection of observations and assessments. The model for selection was that of a 'best fit' for characteristics of learning, aspects of learning and ages/stages of development, as well as meeting the Ofsted requirement to identify children who are falling behind in their learning or who need additional support, and enabling children to make good progress and achieve well.

The nursery schools involved felt that this was not an era where there was funding, or scope for a small team to work full time on the selection of materials for several months. But, taking advantage of the increasing opportunities for collaboration, it was agreed that the selected observations would be shared online as a resource to exemplify *Development Matters*. The materials were launched on the East London Early Years and Schools Partnership website, and linked to the Early Education and Foundation Years websites, with the aim of acting as a prompt for reflection and dialogue in teams of early years practitioners. The initial collection of observations was seen as just the beginning of a work in progress, so the website offers opportunities for feedback, and for practitioners to add new observations and assessments.

Why did nursery schools start this project?

The observation and assessment materials were created as part of a collaborative approach to self-improving systems developed by nursery schools in East London. Successive Ofsted Early Years Reports have shown that some of the highest quality education in the early years sector can be found in nursery schools. In March 2017, 68% of nursery schools were judged outstanding, compared with 19% of all early years providers on non-domestic premises (Ofsted Maintained Schools and Academies Inspections statistics, 2017c). The impact of nursery schools has been particularly strong in the most disadvantaged areas:

> The only early education provision that is at least as strong, or even stronger, in deprived areas compared with wealthier areas is nursery schools. Helpfully, these schools are disproportionately located in deprived areas.
>
> (Ofsted, 2014)

Statutory guidance for local authorities emphasises the role that nursery schools can play in supporting local settings:

> [L]ocal authorities **should** . . . [m]ake full use of their maintained nursery schools, if they have them. Maintained nursery schools are almost

exclusively good or outstanding, the majority are located in disadvantaged areas and they have early years expertise and experience
that can be used to benefit the whole local area. Local authorities
should ensure that they have a role in the pedagogical leadership for
the local early years system. What this means in practice will depend
on local need, but it might include for example: commissioning nursery schools to develop and deliver a quality improvement strategy for
the area; having nursery schools work with other providers to share
their experience and expertise to raise the overall quality of provision
across the area; helping nursery schools to work in partnership with
other providers to offer the 30 hours entitlement; and providing funding to nursery schools to allow them to deliver family support services.

(DfE, 2017, p. 15)

Yet there are only 400 nursery schools left in England, and many are at
risk of closure because the government brought in an Early Years National
Funding Formula that does not take account of the higher cost of employing
teachers in nursery schools. This flies in the face of considerable evidence
that the employment of teachers in nurseries is the most effective indicator
of quality, for example:

EPPE [*Effective Provision of Pre-school Education, 2004*] showed that
quality of settings and child outcomes were higher in settings with
teachers. The higher the proportion of teachers the higher the quality
of learning.

(Professor Iram Siraj, quoting Sylva et al., 2004)

and

[S]tudies consistently show that the presence of trained teachers and
staff with relevant degree-level qualifications in nurseries brings an
added impact for a child's early learning and development, particularly for those growing up in poverty.

(Save the Children, Untapped Potential: How England's nursery
lottery is failing too many children, 2016, p. iv)

Some short-term funding has helped nursery schools stay open, but it is
increasingly clear that they need to play a wider role in supporting the quality

of local settings if they are to survive. Nationally, Ofsted has promoted this approach to quality improvement in the early years sector and schools:

> We'll encourage providers that are good or outstanding to support weaker settings. We know that the best schools are joining forces, and we anticipate that this will happen in the early years.
>
> (Sir Michael Wilshaw, Chief Inspector of Schools and Head of Ofsted, April 2013)

Building on Early Years Teaching Centres and Teaching School Alliances

Two Teaching School Alliances were involved in the development of Celebrating Children's Learning – the East London Early Years and Schools Partnership and the South Thames Early Education Partnership – and across the school sector, Teaching School Alliances have played an important part in professional development and assessing children's learning. However, when teaching schools were first announced by the government in 2010, nursery schools were not eligible to apply for this funding. Pen Green Research Centre – based at Pen Green Nursery School – successfully applied for funding from the Department for Education (DfE) to develop 15 Early Years Teaching Centres across the country in 2011. The Early Years Teaching Centres built on a long tradition of outstanding nursery schools and children's centres supporting local settings and leading on quality improvement. The aim was to share effective practice, support local settings to raise their quality, and improve outcomes for children. The majority of Early Years Teaching Centres went on to become teaching schools or part of Teaching School Alliances when DfE changed the eligibility criteria to include nursery schools in 2013. Celebrating Children's Learning built on the approach developed by the Early Years Teaching Centres and teaching schools.

Learning Without Limits – working together in Newham

The Celebrating Children's Learning process also built on the work of Learning Without Limits, a collaborative network established in 2014 that supports local settings around each of the London Borough of Newham's seven maintained nursery schools. The network grew out of a DfE-funded Early Learning and Community Childcare Hub at Sheringham Nursery School, and improved both the quality of the nursery schools and their local settings through shared good practice, professional dialogue and challenge. All the nursery schools were involved in contributing observations and assessments of children for the Celebrating Children's Learning resources.

The Newham nursery school teams were trained to use the research-evidenced Early Childhood Environmental Rating Scale (ECERS) tools to measure quality at the baseline and end-point of participating settings, and setting and school staff trained together on how to use the data from the audits to draw up plans for improvement. Ofsted outcomes had been poor in the private and voluntary early years sector in Newham at the beginning of the project, and inspection findings identified that the quality of adult-child interactions often required improvement. Mentors from the nursery schools worked with local settings and Newham's Learning and Achievement team to support this process, and Ofsted outcomes for Newham settings improved.

In a further example of this cross-sector approach to improving quality and outcomes for children, Learning Without Limits organises highly successful annual conferences at the University of East London, co-funded by Newham Council. The conferences bring together several hundred early years practitioners from across the sector in Newham and beyond. They have secured world-class researchers and speakers, for example on Sustained Shared Thinking and Emotional Wellbeing (Siraj and Melhuish, 2015) and Wellbeing and Involvement (Laevers, 1994), and held workshops on a wide range of approaches to children's learning. These have included, among others, observations and assessments that celebrate children's learning. Feedback from participants indicates that the learning is transformational.

One important aspect of both the Learning Without Limits network and the Celebrating Children's Learning project is that they have developed a cross-phase approach. Both the network and the project include Kaizen Primary School, which is part of the Newham Reception Innovation Project that brings together school leaders seeking to 'maximise pupil progress through play-based learning in Reception classes'. The project is funded through the Local Authority Innovation Fund and aims to develop effective EYFS leadership skills in schools.

Learning Without Limits works in partnership with, and draws its strength from, the networks around it: Newham's Early Years Team and the East

London Early Years and Schools Partnership (the Teaching School Alliance led by Sheringham Nursery School). It was inspired by the Learning Without Limits project led by the Wroxham School in partnership with Cambridge University, and also drew on the Early Years Teaching Centres approach developed by Pen Green Research Centre. Crucially, the London Borough of Newham has provided funding for the nursery schools to mentor local settings and support their professional development.

In addition, Newham funds one of the nursery schools – Ronald Openshaw Nursery Education Centre – to lead the Special Educational Needs and Disabilities (SEND) hub for the borough. The school co-ordinates the work of the area Special Educational Needs Co-ordinators (SENCOs) who are based there to support inclusion – early identification and assessment – across Newham early years settings (see Chapter 3, 'Valuing and celebrating small steps for children with special educational needs and disabilities: inclusive assessment practice'). This has proved to be a very successful way to integrate the work of the SENCOs with the Learning Without Limits network collaborative approach to quality improvement – and to support inclusive practice across all settings in the borough. The network is also funded by Newham to roll out the Inclusive Classroom Profile, an observation tool designed for settings to evaluate how inclusive they are and how they can improve support for children with special educational needs and disabilities in early childhood settings.

A model for the future?

This integrated approach to shared thinking and developing self-improving systems is now seen as a model for the future in Newham and elsewhere, with local authorities exploring the possibility of basing early years advisory teachers in nursery schools to further integrate their work. In the new world without local authority support for quality improvement in many areas, or the funding to pay for consultants, practitioners have found ways of collaborating, developing their professionalism, and improving the quality of the early education they offer. The Celebrating Children's Learning project grew out of this collaborative (and cost-effective) approach to improving outcomes for children. All the nursery schools and early education consultants who worked to bring together and evaluate observations of children that reflected exciting developments and feelings of wonder did so in their own time, as unpaid volunteers.

We shared a passion for capturing the individuality of each child as they learn, and helping them to become better learners. We also knew that if observations were more personal, and reflected moments of wonder, then parents would feel more engaged and this would support them to feel like partners in encouraging their children's learning. Tania Choudhury's chapter in this book on 'Assessment in diverse contexts: talking with Bangladeshi-British parents about children's early learning' (Chapter 4) demonstrates the importance of listening to parents, understanding the communities they come from, and sharing observations of their children with them at every step of the way. As her chapter shows, the role of parents as their children's first and most consistent educators is well-established in theory, but sharing observations that celebrate children's learning is key to parents engaging with their child's setting and seeing themselves as confident co-educators.

Lesley Webb, in her chapter on 'Celebrating Children's Learning outdoors: a Forest School approach' (Chapter 5), extends this theme further and shows how Forest School can have a profound effect on the way parents view their children, as well as on children's learning, development and health. She discusses a wealth of examples that show how keen observation of children's interests outdoors leads to reviewing and altering plans that help them to develop further.

The nursery schools that developed Celebrating Children's Learning situated this work within a wider ambition of developing a more confident, skilled and professional early years workforce. This fits well with the government's new approach to Assessment without Levels across the school sector, following the removal of national curriculum assessment levels in 2015. The *Final Report on the Commission on Assessment without Levels* made it clear that 'There is no intrinsic value in recording formative assessment; what matters is that it is acted on' (DfE, 2015, p. 6).

This book makes the case for the same approach to be introduced across the early years, and aims to support practitioners, teachers, leaders of education and students to make the change from recording assessments to acting on them. Nursery schools, with their outstanding quality and unique position within both the school and early years sectors, are well placed to play a key role in this transformation.

References

Department for Education (DfE) (2012, revised 2014, 2017) *Early Years Foundation Stage Framework* (Online). www.gov.uk/government/uploads/system/uploads/attachment_data/file/596629/EYFS_STATUTORY_FRAMEWORK_2017.pdf (Last accessed 30 August 2017)

Department for Education (DfE) (2013) *Early Years Outcomes* (Online). www.foundationyears.org.uk/files/2012/03/Early_Years_Outcomes.pdf (Last accessed 30 August 2017)

Department for Education (DfE) (2015) *Final report on the Commission on Assessment without Levels* (Online). www.gov.uk/government/uploads/system/uploads/attachment_data/file/483058/Commission_on_Assessment_without_Levels – report.pdf (Last accessed 27 July 2017)

Department for Education (DfE) (2017) *Early Education and Childcare, Statutory Guidance for Local Authorities* (Online). www.gov.uk/government/uploads/system/uploads/attachment_data/file/351592/early_education_and_childcare_statutory_guidance_2014.pdf (Last accessed 30 August 2017)

Early Education (2012) *Development Matters in the Early Years Foundation Stage (EYFS)* (Online). www.early-education.org.uk/development-matters (Last accessed 31 July 2017)

Laevers, F. (1994) *Defining and Assessing Quality in Early Childhood Education*. Studia Paedagogica, Leuven University Press.

Ofsted (April 2014) *Early Years Annual Report*. London, Bristol, Manchester and Nottingham, UK: Office for Standards in Education, Children's Services and Skills.

Ofsted (2015a) *The Common Inspection Framework: Education, Skills and Early Years*. London, Bristol, Manchester and Nottingham, UK: Office for Standards in Education, Children's Services and Skills.

Ofsted (2015b) *Early Years Inspection Handbook*. London, Bristol, Manchester and Nottingham, UK: Office for Standards in Education, Children's Services and Skills.

Ofsted (2017a) *Childcare Providers and Inspections Main Findings* (Online). www.gov.uk/government/statistics/childcare-providers-and-inspections-as-at-31-march-2017 (Last accessed 30 August 2017)

Ofsted (2017b) *Early Years Inspection: Myths* (Online). www.gov.uk/government/publications/early-years-inspection-handbook-from-september-2015/early-years-inspections-myths (Last accessed 30 August 2017)

Ofsted (2017c) *Maintained Schools and Academies Inspections and Outcomes* (Online). www.gov.uk/government/statistics/maintained-schools-and-academies-inspections-and-outcomes-as-at-31-march-2017 (Last accessed 30 August 2017)

Save the Children (2016) *Untapped Potential: How England's Nursery Lottery Is Failing Too Many Children* (Online). www.savethechildren.org.uk/sites/default/files/docs/Untapped_Potential.pdf (Last accessed 30 August 2017)

Siraj, I., Kingston, D. and Melhuish, E. (2015) *Assessing Quality in Early Childhood Education and Care: Sustained Shared Thinking and Emotional Wellbeing (SSTEW) Scale for 2–5 Year Olds*. London: IOE Press.

Sylva, K., Melhuish, E., Sammons, P., Siraj-Blatchford, I. and Taggart, B. (2004) *The Effective Provision of Pre-School Education (EPPE) Project: Final Report: A Longitudinal Study Funded by the DfES 1997–2004* (Report). Institute of Education, London.

Websites

Early Education: The British Association for Early Years Education (2017) www.early-education.org.uk (Last accessed 31 July 2017)

East London Early Years and Schools Partnership (2017) www.eleysp.co.uk/celebrating-childrens-learning/ (Last accessed 31 July 2017)

Foundation Years: Great Early Years and Childcare (2017) www.foundationyears.org.uk (Last accessed 31 July 2017)

1

Beyond data
Julian Grenier

Introduction

Twenty years ago, I moved from my role as a primary school Early Years co-ordinator to a new position as the Deputy Headteacher of a London nursery school. It was a pioneering integrated centre with babies and toddlers on roll as well as three- and four-year olds, and there were programmes of family support and close, positive links with social workers. My daughter was about a year old and the whole place just felt like it was the 'right place' for children and their families. But I had also unwittingly become a participant in the large-scale Effective Provision of Pre-school Education (EPPE) project (Sylva et al., 2010) and soon found myself being interviewed by one of the researchers. As the questions flowed about children's early learning, assessment, and leading the team, I could hear that much of what I was saying was quite simply nonsense. I have never forgotten that feeling: it dawned on me that I had been busy teaching young children, caring for them, leading a team of practitioners and so on, yet I had never really examined my own theories and ideas.

That is why I now believe strongly that practitioners working in the early years need encouragement and opportunities for reflection and thinking. Early education is not just a programme that anyone can simply be trained to deliver. If we want children to be thinkers, problem-solvers and creators, then we need to prioritise the same attributes in ourselves as practitioners: as Robin Alexander has argued, with reference to primary education, "pupils will not learn to think for themselves if their teachers are expected to do as they are told" (Alexander, 2010, p. 308).

Yet all too often, the actions and decisions taken by early years practitioners are shaped by the tyranny of 'data'. There is little time for practitioners to meet and reflect with senior leaders in schools, or managers in other settings. The precious time that *is* available ends up being dominated, all too often, by discussions about who is 'below expected', where 'the gaps' are, or what proportion of children are going to achieve a 'good level of development'. Parents find themselves receiving baffling tables of data, describing their three-year-olds' development as '16–26 secure' – leaving them wondering what on earth that might mean. Holmes (2015, p. 20) has described this ugly state of affairs as the " 'datafication' of early years teachers and children."

In this chapter, I am going to discuss one of the main findings of the Celebrating Children's Learning project – that we need to go beyond these obscure and dry discussions about 'data'. I will be arguing that good early education can enable children to develop a wider network of relationships, to play, to practise skills, to find multiple ways of communicating and sharing ideas, make new connections and gain new knowledge.

I will be arguing that practitioners need to get to know each child, using 'keen observation' (Dalli et al., 2011), and that in order to notice what is important about children's development and learning, we need to offer a broad, rich and varied curriculum. After all, where there is little for children to do, there will be little for us to notice.

I will be arguing that where there is a rich learning environment and a rich curriculum, practitioners will have more opportunities to find out what children know and can do, how they think and develop their ideas, and what sorts of misconceptions and barriers to learning they might have. This relationship between noticing important things about children and developing effective early education is explored in the next section.

Children as active constructors of their learning

Jan Dubiel (2016, p. 10) makes the important point that "assessment is never an objective activity, nor can it ever be value free." We could not possibly attempt to notice everything about each child in a group: we have to be selective, and one of the ways we are selective is that we draw on our theories about how children learn. We select things that seem to be significant because they tell us about the child's learning and we ignore things that seem to be irrelevant. We should be open about this. As Margaret Carr et al. (2010, p. 20) argue, "early childhood practitioners . . . have to make some assumptions about learning, assessment and evaluation . . . that are informed and reflective."

As Carr's statement implies, learning, assessment and evaluation are all bundled together. You cannot carry out assessments if you are not thinking about learning, and you cannot be an educator and help a child to learn if you are not thinking all of the time about assessment. Learning is not a 'natural' process of development from one stage to another, like a caterpillar morphing into a cocoon and then into a butterfly. Nor is it the case that children have to be taught everything through repetition, reinforcement and practice. The research and evidence is in almost complete agreement: children are active learners and creators of meaning (Evangelou et al., 2009; Dalli et al., 2011; Pascal and Bertram, 2014). Smith (1999, p. 86) puts it neatly when she states that "models of development which emphasise the child's natural and spontaneous development from within or of development as being shaped entirely through learning processes have been strongly criticised." For this reason, commonly used terms like 'tracking children' in early years education are problematic. We could only 'track' children if, as practitioners, we played no role in their learning and development, just as a hunter tracks an animal by following it discreetly rather than helping to guide its journey. Early years practitioners are not just spectators, 'tracking' the child's unfolding development.

The great Russian psychologist Lev Vygotsky (1978) argued that rather than thinking about children in isolation, and merely trying to assess their level of development, we should instead think of children as social learners with a level of development that depends on who they are with. Vygotsky called this the 'zone of proximal development' (or ZPD) and defined it as "the distance between the actual developmental level as determined by independent problem solving and the level of potential development as determined through problem solving under adult guidance, or in collaboration with more capable peers" (Vygotsky, 1978, p. 86). The researchers Wood, Bruner and Ross (1976) famously developed the term 'scaffolding' to describe a pedagogical technique that follows on from Vygotsky's theory. They describe 'scaffolding' as " 'controlling' those elements of the task that are initially beyond the learner's capacity" (Wood, Bruner and Ross, 1976, p. 90).

In other words, we might notice that Ryan has taken his coat off his peg and is then standing slightly frozen, unsure of what to do next, and jot down the observation that "Ryan can't put his coat on." Or we might notice Ryan is stuck, and use the pedagogical technique of 'scaffolding'. We could say something like, "If I hold your coat, can you put your arm in?" or "If I start off the zip, can you pull it up to the top?" This encourages Ryan to do things that he is able to do, whilst we do the things he cannot – we manage those elements of the task of putting on a coat that are currently beyond his ability.

A similar approach can be taken to developing a conversation with a child. If we spend time getting to know children, then we can help them with those parts of the conversation that might otherwise end in a roadblock. When Fatima comes up to her key person and says *"noo-noo gone way,"* her key person knows that *'noo-noo'* is her pet name for her auntie and is able to keep the conversation going by saying, *"Oh, where has aunty Tasmin gone?"* This is what the researchers in the Oxford Pre-School Project, a study of early education in Oxfordshire in the 1970s, call a 'contingent' response to a child.

Wood, McMahon and Cranstoun (1980) make the distinction between the 'contingent' and the 'programmatic' responses adults make to children. A 'contingent' response depends on the adult knowing the child: "the adult takes the child's interests and ideas as a focus and maintains the interaction contingently rather than programmatically" (Wood, McMahon and Cranstoun, 1980, p. 205). So Fatima's key person works hard, drawing on her knowledge, to develop a conversation about auntie Tasmin and does not simply say, *"Lovely, Fatima, now it's circle time, be a good girl and sit down."* A very shocking example of a 'programmatic' response to a child, from the Oxford Pre-School Project, is described by Garland and White (1980, p. 53): "a child bursts out with the comment that *'my Daddy's dead, but I've got a grandfather and he's going to take me to school'*, only for the practitioner to reply *'is he?'"* and then continue "asking the children to recite in turn *'it-is-Wednesday-the-thirtieth-of-June-hot-and-sunny'*."

During the EPPE project, the researchers built on this concept of the 'contingent response' and described a new pedagogical technique that they dubbed 'sustained shared thinking' (SST). In *Researching Pedagogy in the Early Years* (Siraj-Blatchford et al., 2002), sustained shared thinking is described as "an episode in which two or more individuals 'work together' in an intellectual way to solve a problem, clarify a concept, evaluate activities, extend a narrative etc. Both parties must contribute to the thinking and it must develop and extend." More recently, Siraj, Kingston and Melhuish (2015) have added the clarifications that SST does not have to involve an adult-child dialogue, but might happen when children are talking with each other, and that it "may include 'standing back' and allowing the child to explore, familiarize, solve problems, and think by themselves or in pairs as well as intervening and supporting the child." The EPPE researchers also use the term 'reflexive co-construction' (Siraj-Blatchford et al., 2002) to describe the type of effective early years pedagogy that is characterised by taking children's ideas as the starting point for extended and mutual investigation.

In this section, I have argued that children are active constructors of their learning. Effective practitioners develop conversations and shared activities with children by using the pedagogical techniques of scaffolding, responding contingently to what children say, and developing sustained shared thinking. These ideas should directly inform how we think about assessment in the early years. If practitioners always stand back, or if they are constantly trying to note down a child's 'significant learning', then it is unlikely that they are engaging in extended discussion, shared thinking, or scaffolding. In fact, the pressure to 'gather evidence' and to assess will directly interfere with their capacity to support the children's learning. It is little wonder that Osgood (2012, p. 127) found that 'doing observations' is experienced as a laborious chore by many staff working with young children.

Mountains of evidence

As previously outlined, the best practice in early years assessment is in line with what we know about how young children learn, and how adults can best teach them. When practitioners practise 'keen observation', they can quickly adapt their approach to scaffold the child's learning and help the child practise a skill, learn something new, develop an idea or overcome a difficulty.

When a four-year-old girl at Sheringham Nursery School was recently experimenting with different materials in our WaterPlay Zone, she saw a small stone sink rapidly to the bottom of the tray and told the practitioner that *"heavy things go to the bottom."* Seeing an opportunity to develop her scientific thinking, the practitioner asked, *"I wonder what will happen if we put the stone on the boat?"* The stone was placed on a plastic boat and, to the child's surprise, the boat with the stone on it floated. The practitioner then pushed down on the boat and encouraged the child to do the same: she commented, *"It feels like the water's pushing my hand."* They continued to discuss what they observed and felt, and the practitioner resisted the temptation to rush the child towards any conclusions. It was a very skilfully supported episode of joint investigation and sustained shared thinking. By way of contrast, I can remember how in my own reception class, some years ago, I wrote a label on a display that said "we investigated floating and sinking and we found that heavy things sink." When the Local Authority Science Advisory Teacher visited, she ruefully commented, *"Better not get on that ferry to France this year, then."*

Effective early years teaching, which rests on keen observation and quick responses to what children are doing and saying, dissolves the perceived boundary between 'adult-directed teaching' and 'child-initiated learning'. As Bruner (1995, p. 6) argues, this type of teaching involves "adults treating the child as an agent and bent on 'teaching' him to be more so." The more children develop their thinking, skills and understanding, the more they can be agents in early years settings and reception classes. They become more able to make their own choices and follow through their decisions. Just as effective teaching promotes more autonomy in early learning, Kochanska et al. (2001, cited in Evangelou et al., 2009, p. 19) have also argued that close and emotionally attuned caregiving helps children to become more autonomous: "the child embraces the caregiver's agenda, and thus experiences compliance as self-generated and not interfering with striving for autonomy" leading to "voluntary, thoughtful adaptive and effective self-regulation." The evidence suggests that effective practice in both teaching and caring for young children makes them more autonomous, stronger and better able to self-regulate.

However, if practitioners are under pressure to collect and collate huge amounts of evidence, then their ability to work in these ways is severely constrained. Writing a post-it note that "Jason likes playing with the blocks" or snapping a photo of a smiling Jason next to a tower of unit blocks he has built might capture his enjoyment. But it will make no contribution to his early education. And constantly jotting down notes and taking photos interferes with the time and availability of practitioners to provide the emotionally attuned care and rich, stimulating interactions that children need to thrive. Bradbury (2012, p. 179) comments that "during classroom observations, I noted that the accumulation of evidence was a time-consuming process which dominated much of classroom life: teachers would constantly write notes, fill in charts and take photographs, while teaching assistants spent many hours each week sticking observations into individual children's folders."

Perhaps as worryingly, this culture is having a seriously negative effect on practitioners' sense of professional self-worth and creating unsustainable workloads. Bradbury (2012, p. 179) vividly relates how Jim, a reception teacher, describes the "pressure to collect evidence at the beginning of the year: 'You've got 22 folders down there with nothing in and it's like, Christ, let's fill it. You need stuff in there – we need to show that we're doing work'."

Building on interests and filling gaps

As I have argued, the piles of photographs stuck into folders, post-it notes in files, and the updates on cloud-based learning journeys can needlessly take up practitioners' time and make them feel overwhelmed. What is worse, much of this mountain of evidence often remains unread and unthought about. All of that information serves merely to 'evidence' that the practitioners – and children – are getting lots done, and it gets in the way of the real business of playing with children, developing conversations, and exploring ideas and thinking.

However, 'evidence' of this sort is sometimes used either to identify children's interests or to highlight 'gaps' in their learning. But both of these uses lead to ineffective approaches to early years education.

As previously described, it is important to get to know children, and find out what their interests are, if practitioners are going to be able to respond in a 'contingent' manner to their play and to what they say. But it is possible for this process to be taken too far. When provision largely follows on from children's identified interests, there is a danger that children who have not had a wide range of experiences might find themselves given a rather restricted diet of 'more of the same'. It could hardly be judged a success if the child who starts their nursery year interested in riding the trikes and dressing up as Spiderman ends the year going round and round on the same trike and occasionally putting a cloak on and pretending to fire off some webs. As Margaret Donaldson argues:

> Education is about changing lives . . . It is about changing the modal repertoire for one thing. It is about suggesting new directions in which lives may go.
>
> (2002, cited in Carr et al., 2010, p. 17)

When the practitioners in the East London Partnership's Outstanding Early Years Teaching group visited Wentworth Nursery School and Children's Centre in Hackney, it was striking to see how children's disparate interests in superhero play had been skilfully brought together by a practitioner who, one morning, faced them with a planet-saving emergency that required each superhero to solve a problem using their super-powers. The whole morning was brilliantly captured in a large floor-book, including the children's own words, pretend play sequences, and (in some cases) drawing and writing. So the children's mode of play was hugely widened from simple copying and re-enactment into more flexible pretend play, negotiation and problem-solving. It is worth noting, at this point, that evidence from the research of Blair and Raver (2015) shows a strong association between participation in this type of complex, socio-dramatic play and the development of self-regulation, which, in turn, is a powerful predictor of children's later success in school.

Similarly, when all of the three- and four-year olds from Sheringham Nursery School had a day at the beach, their teacher was determined that this would be more than a lovely day out for children, parents and staff (important though that was). Ruby was absolutely fascinated by the stones on the Essex shore and spent much of the day holding them, stacking them up, throwing them into the sea, and talking about them. She filled her pockets with them and brought them back with her. So her teacher ensured that there were many stones available for her to explore the next day in the nursery, in addition to those Ruby had collected during the trip. Practitioners have an important responsibility to widen children's experiences – in Ruby's case, both by taking her somewhere new and wonderful to her (the beach) and by helping her to extend her investigation into a different mode, expressing herself artistically with the stones. Her teacher noted:

> When we returned to nursery your play centred around the pebbles. You had been so fascinated by experiencing stones in huge numbers on the beach that you played with them for most of the session and revisited them regularly over the week. Some of the pebbles were ones we had collected together from Chalkwell beach. Others were polished, white, or much bigger, from the nursery collection.
> You grouped together smaller pebbles and enclosed them with larger stones. You also experimented with raising the stones up on platforms and enclosing the logs with stones to create flower shapes.

You balanced smaller stones on top of pebbles, which was tricky as the surface was not always flat.

You had brought one of your Barbie shoes in from home. It appeared on all of your sculptures because it was so special to you.

You really wanted to record this on the iPad because it was such a significant experience for you, saying "Please print these up and put them in my special book, now!" You used the iPad independently to capture this moment.

As I argued in the beginning of this chapter, effective early education rests on the provision of a rich, broad and balanced curriculum. But we need to be wary that we do not interpret 'balance' to mean that we analyse observational evidence to find 'gaps' and then distort the curriculum to 'fill the gaps'. If children are hardly ever noticed taking part in expressive arts and design activities, perhaps we need to question whether the provision is engaging enough rather than herd children to a painting table to make sure that a gap in the evidence is plugged.

Nancy Stewart, who co-wrote the non-statutory guidance to the Early Years Foundation Stage, recently noted that when *Development Matters* is "used as a tick list of descriptors of what children must achieve, it can sadly limit both children's development and the professional awareness and skills of practitioners" (Stewart, 2016). No one would argue that planning for early learning should be reduced to a list of gaps to fill or empty boxes that need a tick in them. Yet that can be exactly what happens, when misguided assessment systems drive planning and provision.

In any case, I would suggest that we should not be excessively concerned about children's desire to go deeper and to specialise at a young age. Nor should we be surprised or worried if they swerve away at times from certain areas of the curriculum. That is what young children are like: they learn in ways that are sometimes complex and unpredictable. Acquiring a great deal of knowledge about the names and categories of dinosaurs, spending many hours outdoors searching for worms and snails, or playing out endless variations of *Whatever Next* can all be very rich contexts for further learning and development. In support of this argument, Carr et al. (2010, p. 32) describe how "Mihaly Csikszentmihalyi (1996) interviewed ninety-one 'creative' people (including fourteen Nobel Prize winners) and concluded that in their early years those innovative thinkers had at least one strongly developed interest (even if this was not the interest that they became known for later in life)."

Developing high-quality practice

One part of the problem with observation and assessment practice in the early years concerns the uses, and abuses, of the information that is being gathered. Another equally important problem is that the information being collected can be of poor quality. When the Celebrating Children's Learning project team looked at the strongest practice gathered together – and there were examples from all of the participating schools – we found that each example had some or all of the following attributes:

- You can 'hear' the child's voice or 'get a feel' for their play.
- There is keen observation of the child's exploration, play and thinking.
- The practitioner has noticed that the child is learning a new skill, or is making new links between aspects of knowledge.
- There are examples of sustained shared thinking, or a response from the child showing their feeling of awe and wonder.

On the other hand, examples of weaker practice tended either to restate wording from *Development Matters* (Early Education, 2012) or to give vague information about what children are doing.

Here are two contrasting examples concerning a young child called Serena in the under-twos provision of a maintained nursery school. Her key person notices that Serena is already aware of some of the routines of the day, like tidying up, and is beginning to understand how to participate in them. Serena is only saying a few words, but she initiates a dialogue with Cathy, the practitioner. The observational record is written so that it is addressed to Serena, which strengthens the sense that the child is a co-constructor of meaning in the nursery:

> *Serena, I watched you today interacting with Cathy in the graphics area. You were watching Cathy putting pencils in a cup and you picked up one with your left hand and mirrored what Cathy did before. Serena, you continued doing this until most of the pencils were collected. When you saw one pencil left on the table you pointed to it with your eye gaze to Cathy. She gave it to you and you took it with your left hand and put it in the cup.*

This 'keen observation' is brief, but rich in detail: it tells us so much about Serena's understanding, her desire to participate and her ability to communicate. Dalli et al. comment that "to see the infant and toddler as a learner still constitutes a challenging paradigmatic shift for many teachers" (Dalli et al., 2011, p. 18): it is clear that the practitioners working with Serena have engaged with that challenge and are fully aware of how care and other routines for children up to the age of two can be opportunities for the children's thinking and learning.

On the other hand, just a few pages away was an observation that stated, *"Serena, you have started to build a special relationship with me as your key person + other peers."* Written notes like these are common in children's folders – I have probably written hundreds in my time, and I have certainly seen hundreds in my work with schools and settings. They tell us next to nothing about children, and so they are of no use either in getting to know a child or thinking about how to help the child's learning.

Celebrating Children's Learning sharpened our awareness at Sheringham Nursery School of how we might develop our practice further. Alison Peacock (2016) makes the important point that it is through dialogue that we can begin to understand a child's emerging development and understanding. Sometimes, it is possible to have that dialogue directly with a young child in the early years, and other times the dialogue will be conducted by practitioners with parents, or between practitioners. But, in all cases, it is only observations like the first example about Serena that can prompt dialogue because they give us something to talk about: they tell us about how the child learns, and about their 'learning capacity' (Peacock, 2016, p. 18).

However, working together to ensure that this type of practice became consistent across the whole team – which is made up of staff at many different levels of qualification and experience – was difficult. There was already a long-established culture that assessment information at Sheringham was not 'high stakes' – for example, performance management would not put pressure on staff to produce data as evidence for pre-specified performance outcomes. A lot of emphasis was placed on professional trust. The most important assessment information was in children's 'Special Books': these are large A3 books with photos, samples of children's mark-making, and observational notes that children can revisit daily, and are taken home so that families can add to them. Yet although this approach is much-loved by staff, many said they experienced a great deal of pressure around the management of so much observation and assessment information.

Helen Currie, the nursery school's assistant headteacher, developed a cycle of support and coaching for staff that was carefully planned to help members of the team build on what they were already doing well, and to help them become more able to make autonomous, informed decisions about what to record and how to use the information. At the same time, we made decisions as a team to reduce the quantity of information we were collecting, and to simplify its analysis. This is discussed briefly in the next section, which is titled "The 'datafication' of the early years."

The first, important intervention Helen made was to explore why some staff felt overwhelmed by the workload, and to work alongside them to generate solutions. Some aspects of our assessment system were dropped, and others were reduced. Staff also shared practical strategies for making the best use of the time they had away from the children. For example, it helped greatly if a member of staff had time to discuss their thoughts about a child before they spent time on their own entering information into a child's Special Book.

We also explored how team planning meetings could feel very pressured. At Sheringham, each team is led by a class teacher and includes three or more early years educators (with a level 3 qualification in Childcare and Education). Team members found it a challenge to complete the planning that was needed for the week, and when we reflected more deeply, it also became clear that little time was spent on what should be the most important team activity – discussing children's learning and thinking about teaching. A team meeting provides a special opportunity to gain multiple perspectives on a child's development: a key person might feel that their child is getting really 'stuck', only to find that someone else in the team has achieved a real breakthrough elsewhere in the provision. After a careful analysis of the topics of discussion in team meetings, Sheringham's Deputy Headteacher (Lesley Webb) suggested a refocus, with staff bringing high-quality observations of children's learning for discussion and debate. The main focus of the meeting would be dialogue about learning, with the teachers ensuring that over time, no child was left out, and that more time was spent talking about children who may be vulnerable. The teachers would then develop the week's planning out of those rich discussions, and plans would be updated daily in response to the children's learning and interests. It was important that those high-quality observations were shared, discussed and acted on: for as the *Final Report of the Commission for Assessment without Levels* states (Department for Education, 2015, p. 30), "there is no intrinsic value in recording formative assessment; what matters is that it is acted on."

But assuring the quality of the observations that were brought to the meeting was not simple. We wanted each observation to be as precise as possible about the child's learning, communication and progress (or barriers to progress). In this way, we aimed to make learning more visible to parents, staff and to the children themselves. To help the team work towards these aims, Helen organised writing workshops with team members so we could practise ways of explaining that a child is just beginning to do something, is developing in their confidence and competence, or has now mastered a skill or can make connections between ideas. Helen summarised this learning in an aide-memoire that was shared with all staff, generated from our work together. The key focus was on the Characteristics of Effective Learning, which staff said they found most difficult to write about, with a briefer section about words and phrases to use that highlight children's progress (see Tables 1.1–1.6).

At the end of the year, one of the Special Book entries that we felt exemplified the changes we wanted to achieve was about Jamal's determination to make a party hat. The description of Jamal's activity is skilfully written, not only to give rich detail about his problem-solving and about the shared,

Table 1.1 Playing and exploring – engagement

	Words for playing and exploring – engagement
Finding out and exploring • Showing curiosity about objects, events and people • Using senses to explore the world around them • Engaging in open-ended activity • Showing particular interests	Curious, explored, investigated, engaged, interested in, excited by, discovered, took a risk, trial and error, effort, challenge, practiced, had a go, pretended, represented, took on a role, initiated, combined, were interested in, built, concentrated, persisted
Playing with what they know • Pretending objects are things from their experience • Representing their experiences in play • Taking on a role in their play • Acting out experiences with other people	
Being willing to 'have a go' • Initiating activities • Seeking challenge • Showing a 'can do' attitude • Taking a risk, engaging in new experiences and learning by trial and error	

Table 1.2 Active learning – motivation

	Words for active learning – motivation
Being involved and concentrating • Maintaining focus on their activity for a period of time • Showing high levels of energy, fascination • Not easily distracted • Paying attention to details	Focused, (period of time)___minutes, fascinated, energy, paid attention/not distracted, persisted, challenge, changed, recovered, satisfied, achieved, proud, accomplished, stimulated, made goals, made plans, effort, learnt, motivated, deeply involved, curious, maintained focus
Keeping on trying • Persisting with activity when challenges occur • Showing a belief that more effort or a different approach will pay off • Bouncing back after difficulties	
Enjoying achieving what they set out to do • Showing satisfaction in meeting their own goals • Being proud of how they accomplished something – not just the end result • Enjoying meeting challenges for their own sake rather than external rewards or praise	

Table 1.3 Creating and critical thinking

	Words for creating and critical thinking
Having their own ideas • Thinking of ideas • Finding ways to solve problems • Finding new ways to do things	Thought, wondered, maybe, knew, remembered, forgot, idea, made sense, planned, learnt, found out, confused, figured out what you were trying to do, puzzled, what else was possible, talked aloud, described, interested, created, met a challenge, problem-resolution, solved problems, patterns, links, new ways to do things, predicted, tested, developed, sequenced, cause and effect, decision, reached a goal, strategy, changed, reviewed, were flexible
Making links • Making links and noticing patterns in their experience • Making predictions • Testing their ideas • Developing ideas of grouping, sequences, cause and effect	
Choosing ways to do things • Planning, making decisions about how to approach a task, solve a problem and reach a goal • Checking how well their activities are going • Changing strategy as needed • Reviewing how well the approach worked	

Table 1.4 Writing about progress – emerging

The first time you tried . . . At first . . . You started . . . In the beginning . . . When you first . . . Initially . . . You began . . . Unsure . . . Tried . . . Tested . . . Nervously . . . Suddenly . . . Short periods . . . Frustrated . . . Novice . . . Concentrated hard . . .

Table 1.5 Writing about progress – practising and repeating

The next time . . . Again . . . You carried on . . . Next you . . . When you revisited . . . You continued . . . Tried again . . . Once more . . . Happy to . . . Repeated . . . Happy . . . Confidently . . . Better than before . . . Longer period . . . Concentrated . . .

Table 1.6 Writing about progress – mastery

Finally . . . Always . . . Continued . . . Revisited . . . Happy to . . . Expertly . . . Developed . . . Showed others how to . . . Supported others . . . Now you can . . . Moved onto . . . A long time . . . Happy to . . . Relaxed . . . Mastered . . . Could do this whilst doing something else . . . Combine this with something else . . . Make links with another idea or experience . . .

sustained thinking between him and the practitioner, but also to show the progress he is making. It is clear where he is revisiting and practising difficult skills, like cutting, and where he is close to mastery of a skill, for example in writing his name. The dialogue between Jamal and the practitioner gives important insights into his understanding and his learning dispositions.

> *Jamal, after Christmas you came back to nursery and wanted to make a party hat that you remembered from before the holiday. You had a clear idea of how you wanted to make it. You drew a zig-zag line across the paper and cut along it.*
>
> *You asked me, "Will it be big enough?" I helped you to hold it around your head. It was too small. You asked me, "How can I make it bigger?"*
>
> *We thought about this together. I suggested a strip of paper, but you said, "No, I'm going to make some more." So you cut out another one the same as the first and you stuck the two parts together. You persisted for a long time with this tricky cutting. You asked for help to test whether the crown would fit, and it did.*

You said, "I'm going to write my name." It was the first time you did this without looking at your name card.

When you finished, you tried it on. You said to me, "Take my picture, so I can see myself." Then you put the hat on my head and used the camera to take a photo of me. "It doesn't really fit you," you said.

As I have argued, it is important to recognise that what we notice about children's learning is intertwined with how we can best teach them. When we are highly observant about children – noticing Serena's response to tidying-up time, or Jamal's efforts to make a party hat – we can scaffold their development and help them to do things they could not accomplish alone. Capturing this is not a simple task: if we are committed to developing high-quality approaches to assessment, then we need to offer support, coaching and practical help to our teams. We want to be committed to learning together in a climate of professional trust.

Yet instead of focussing on improving the quality and effectiveness of early years education, there has been much more emphasis in many schools and settings on the collection of massive quantities of data about children. This is discussed in the next section.

The 'datafication' of the early years

In the previous section, I have outlined some of the ways that the Sheringham team have worked to make children's progress in their learning more visible. As Dubiel (2016, p. 14) argues, "although it is quite possible and reasonable to describe and articulate the 'progress' that all children make, this should not be compromised by applying a simplistic formula for ease of expression." Assessment in the early years should be principled and responsible: it should promote the best interests of children, and not be distorted by this desire for 'ease of expression'.

The most common distortion arises from a desire to evidence progress and 'value added'. This means that children's attainment on entry is still, in far too many cases, artificially depressed. Schools and settings all over the country – even those in affluent areas – continue to report that on entry, children's levels of development are 'below the expected levels'. There are three obvious problems with this.

First, there is no clarity about what is 'expected' in children's development when they start in a nursery or in a reception class. Some of the children may be 11 months older than others when they begin (the difference between the youngest summer-born children and the older autumn-born in the same school year). Should we reasonably assume that a child who has just turned four years old will have the same level of development as a child who is four years and 11 months old? In any case, whilst *Development Matters* (Early Education, 2012) gives an overview of how children may develop, it is not based on any evidence about what a child aged between 40–60 months should be able to do. No robust, large-scale surveys of child development underpin *Development Matters* (ibid) – it is simply intended as guidance.

Second, it cannot be true that the development of more-or-less every child in England is below the level expected for their age. Yet in my work with settings and schools, this is the ubiquitous description of children's development on entry. As Ofsted (2014) has argued, accurate assessment of children should be a collaborative effort involving parents and (if applicable) the previous setting or childminder. We should be trying to find out as much as we can about a child's development – not marking them down as low as we can.

Third, depressing assessment levels on entry – whether children start in nursery setting or reception class – may make it easier to show progress or 'value added', but it also has a corrosive effect. It lowers practitioners' expectations. When I recently heard that a school leader was asking staff to lower their assessments so that the children had *"room to grow and we can show our value-added,"* it struck me that those children were unlikely to get the sort of challenging provision they need in order to become more engaged, creative and persistent learners. It also strikes me that the very application of the term 'value added' to children's education is problematic. The Oxford English Dictionary (2017) defines the term as "the amount by which the value of an article is increased at each stage of its production, exclusive of initial costs." The concept has travelled from economics to education, but I would argue that it should have been stopped at the border – children are not economic units of value whose worth can be added to, but people who make choices and have agency about their learning, and who come from families and communities who also play a role in their development.

An excessive focus on data and tracking levels within *Development Matters* is having the same negative effect as the narrow assessment of levels in Key Stages One and Two had in the past. The Commission on Assessment without Levels commented that "levels also used a 'best fit' model, which meant that a pupil could have serious gaps in their knowledge and understanding, but still be placed within the level. This meant it wasn't always clear exactly which areas of the curriculum the child was secure in and where the gaps were" (Department for Education, 2015, p. 12). Assessment practices in the early years still run that risk. Two children might be given a 'best fit' assessment that they are working within the 30–50 month band for numbers at the end of their nursery year. But each child may have a very different level of understanding, and different gaps in their knowledge. The assessment serves the purpose of summarising the children's level and demonstrating their progress. But it fails to help the child's next teacher understand what sort of planning and provision each child needs to continue their learning.

Finally, there are other popularly used systems to generate data that can be equally problematic because they are not consistent with the evidence base about children's learning and effective teaching in the early years. One example is the collation of scores showing children's involvement in their learning (Laevers, 1994; Laevers et al., 2011). The usefulness of this approach and the data it generates has been robustly challenged by the EPPE researchers who argue that measuring children's involvement "provides no basis for assessing the content of the engagement e.g. to what extent the teacher's intervention may be considered 'worthwhile' or, with regard to 'content', whether the 'correct' information is imparted" (Siraj-Blatchford et al., 2002).

However, it is important to stress that I am not arguing that there is *no* role for data about children's development and progress in early years education. Peacock (2016, p. 100) usefully explains how, as the headteacher of Wroxham School, she used data about children's learning proportionately: "we only used tracking as a failsafe background metric to ensure that every child's learning was noticed as opposed to using tracking to hold individual teachers to account or to report in-year or end of year grades to children and families."

Without sharp analysis of assessment information, practitioners will be unable to address very basic questions of equality: Are some groups of children thriving more in our provision than others? Are there some children who may be at risk of making poor progress? Tools to analyse assessment information can help us to consider such questions, but I would argue that the data produced needs to be considered in the round, alongside other metrics, like robust quality assurance tools, the professional knowledge of the staff working directly with the children, and the insights of the parents. For these reasons, Sheringham Nursery School worked with the educational consultant James Pembroke and chose to adopt a system of data management that was easy to use and easy to customise, called Insight.

It is important that we do not fool ourselves: inequality remains a critical problem in English society, and early years education is an important part of the whole civic structure that should be acting in the best interests of every child. There are always questions to ask about the testing and ranking of young children, but I would argue it would be simple foolishness to ignore challenges like the following one highlighted in Ofsted's *Unseen Children* report:

> In the UK, for example, large gaps exist in the results from vocabulary tests between children from middle and low income families. Children from low income backgrounds in the UK are 19 months behind their better off peers compared with only 10.6 months in Canada.
>
> (Ofsted, 2013, p. 37)

Identifying a possible problem is important, but then it is important to act intelligently on the best available information – not merely gather even more data.

I would argue that practitioners need a range of sources of information from within their provision, and from beyond. At Sheringham Nursery School, information about children's progress can be found in many places including their Special Books, in the dialogue with parents, in the dialogue in planning meetings, from children's own reflections, and from the analysis of outcomes provided by Insight. Along with the New Zealand researchers Mitchell and Cubey, I would argue in favour of professional development and learning opportunities for early years practitioners that are characterised by "understandable data that reveals 'pedagogy in action' and others' views . . . Professional development is linked to tangible changes in pedagogical interactions and this in turn is associated with children's learning in early childhood settings. The professional development helps participants to change educational practice, beliefs, understanding, and/or attitudes" (Mitchell and Cubey, 2003, p. xii).

So, continuing the focus on children's early communication, which is absolutely fundamental to their learning, we know a great deal about what works. To summarise, effective practice includes:

• Creating a rich and stimulating learning environment, in which children experience a high quality of care

- Prioritising the importance of adults getting to know each child as an individual, so that they can respond contingently to what children say
- Scaffolding children's learning through reflexive co-construction and sustained shared thinking
- Providing contexts for children to develop their self-regulation, including an emphasis on high-quality care, and on opportunities for pretend play

The only role that generating and analysing assessment information and other data can usefully play in early years education is to check whether we are working towards this sort of high-quality provision, and whether it is effective for each individual child. But the power to change things for children, for the better, lies in our hands as practitioners:

> As Snow, Tabors and Dickinson (2001) have shown, extended discourse and exposure to rich vocabulary in the home is a strong predictor of early elementary language and literacy growth and as I have argued elsewhere (Siraj-Blatchford, 2009), these practices are ubiquitous in middle class, western family contexts, but they can't be taken for granted elsewhere. The EPPE research (Siraj-Blatchford and Sylva, 2004) provides only one of the most recent contributions to a growing body of evidence that shows that there are many disadvantaged children in even the wealthiest of countries that deserve our very best pedagogical efforts when they attend pre-school settings.
>
> (Siraj-Blatchford, 2009, p. 87)

Now is the right moment for all of us – practitioners, leaders and managers – to be much bolder. We need to resist the 'datafication' of the early years, and focus instead on improving the quality and depth of our assessment practices. We need to ensure that our assessment practices support us in making our very best pedagogical efforts, rather than getting in the way and overwhelming us.

Every day, children in the early years show huge courage in their learning: they put something unfamiliar in their mouths and taste it, they wobble and fall off two-wheeled bikes, they try and try again to write their name or to build a tower that is higher than they are. Surely, it is time for us to show the same courage in our practice, and to do the right thing for children?

References

Alexander, R. J. (ed.) (2010) *Children, Their World, Their Education: Final Report and Recommendations of the Cambridge Primary Review*. Oxford: Routledge.

Blair, C. and Raver, C. C. (2015) School readiness and self-regulation: A developmental psychobiological approach. *Annual Review of Psychology*, 66, 711–731.

Bradbury, A. (2012) "I feel absolutely incompetent": Professionalism, policy and early childhood teachers. *Contemporary Issues in Early Childhood*, 13, 175–186.

Bruner, J. (1995) From joint attention to meeting of minds: An introduction. In C. Moore and P. J. Dunham (eds.), *Joint Attention: Its Origins and Role in Development*. Hillsdale, NJ: Lawrence Erlbaum Associates.

Carr, M., Lee, W., Jones, C., Smith, A., Marshall, K. and Duncan, J. (2010) *Learning in the Making: Disposition and Design in Early Education*. Boston: Sense Publishers.

Dalli, C., White, E., Rockel, J. and Duhn, I. (2011) Quality early childhood education for under-two-year-olds: What should it look like? *A Literature Review* (Online). http://thehub.superu.govt.nz/sites/default/files/41442_QualityECE_Web-22032011_0.pdf (Last accessed 27 July 2017)

Department for Education (2015) *Final Report of the Commission on Assessment without Levels* (Online). www.gov.uk/government/uploads/system/uploads/attachment_data/file/483058/Commission_on_Assessment_Without_Levels_-_report.pdf (Last accessed 27 July 2017)

Dubiel, J. (2016) *Effective Assessment in the Early Years Foundation Stage* (2nd ed.). London: Sage.

Early Education (2012) *Development Matters in the Early Years Foundation Stage* (Online). www.early-education.org.uk/development-matters (Last accessed 27 July 2017)

Evangelou, M., Sylva, K., Kyriacou, M., Wild, M. and Glenny, G. (2009) *Early Years Learning and Development Literature Review* (Online). www.foundationyears.org.uk/wp-content/uploads/2012/08/DCSF-RR1761.pdf (Last accessed 27 July 2017)

Garland, C. and White, S. (1980) *Children and Day Nurseries: Management and Practice in Nine London Day Nurseries*. London: Grant McIntyre.

Holmes, G. (2015) The "datafication" of early years pedagogy: "If the teaching is good, the data should be good and if there's bad teaching, there is bad data". *Journal of Education Policy*, 30 (3), 1–13.

Laevers, F. (1994) *An Exploration of the Concept of Involvement as an Indicator for Quality in Early Childhood Education*. Dundee: Scottish Consultative Council on the Curriculum.

Laevers, F., Declercq, B., Marin, C., Moons, J. and Stanton, F. (2011) *Observing Involvement in Children From Birth to 6 Years*. DVD and Manual. http://earlyexcellence.com/

Mitchell, L. and Cubey, P. (2003). *Characteristics of Effective Professional Development Linked to Enhanced Pedagogy and Children's Learning in Early Childhood Settings: Best Evidence Synthesis* (Online). http://www.educationcounts.govt.nz/publications/curriculum/2515/5955 (Last accessed 22 July, 2017)

Ofsted (2013) *Unseen Children: Access and Achievement 20 Years On* (Online). www.gov.uk/government/uploads/system/uploads/attachment_data/file/379157/Unseen_20children_20-_20access_20and_20achievement_2020_20years_20on.pdf (Last accessed 27 July 2017)

Ofsted (2014) *Are You Ready: Good Practice in School Readiness* (Online). www.gov.uk/government/uploads/system/uploads/attachment_data/file/418819/Are_you_ready_Good_practice_in_school_readiness.pdf (Last accessed 27 July 2017)

Osgood, J. (2012) *Narratives From the Nursery: Negotiating Professional and Identities in Early Childhood*. London: Routledge.

Oxford English Dictionary (2017) (Online) https://en.oxforddictionaries.com/ (Last accessed 27 July 2017)

Pascal, C. and Bertram, T. (2014) *Early Years Literature Review* (Online). www.early-education.org.uk/sites/default/files/CREC%20Early%20Years%20Lit%20Review%202014%20for%20EE.pdf (Last accessed 27 July 2017)

Peacock, A. (2016) *Assessment for Learning without Limits*. London: Open University Press.

Siraj-Blatchford, I. (2009) Conceptualising progression in the pedagogy of play and sustained shared thinking in early childhood education: A Vygotskian perspective. *Education and Child Psychology*, 26 (2), 77–89.

Siraj-Blatchford, I., Kingston, D. and Melhuish, E. (2015) *Assessing Quality in Early Childhood Education and Care: Sustained Shared Thinking and Emotional Well-Being (SSTEW) Scale for 2–5-Year-Olds Provision*. London: IOE Press.

Siraj-Blatchford, I., Sylva, K., Muttock, S., Gilden, R. and Bell, D. (2002) *Researching Effective Pedagogy in the Early Years*. London: Department for Education and Skills.

Smith, A. (1999) Quality childcare and joint attention. *International Journal of Early Years Education*, 7 (1), 85–98.

Stewart, N. (2016) *Development Matters: A Landscape of Possibilities, Not a Roadmap* (Online). http://eyfs.info/articles/_/teaching-and-learning/development-matters-a-landscape-of-possibilit-r205 (Last accessed 27 July 2017)

Sylva, K., Melhuish, E., Sammons, P., Siraj-Blatchford, I. and Taggart, B. (eds.) (2010) *Early Childhood Matters: Evidence From the Effective Pre-School and Primary Education Project*. London: Routledge.

Vygotsky, L. (1978) *Mind in Society: The Development of Higher Psychological Processes*. London: Harvard University Press.

Wood, D., Bruner, J. and Ross, G. (1976) The role of tutoring in problem solving. *Journal of Child Psychology and Psychiatry*, 17, 89–100.

Wood, D., McMahon, L. and Cranstoun, Y. (1980) *Working With Under Fives*. London: Grant McIntyre.

2

Putting the Characteristics of Effective Learning at the heart of assessment

Nancy Stewart and Helen Moylett

Let us start with a story:

> *Aymeline has got a large [piece of] fabric. She gives it to Mariam and says, "Let's play camels". They go under the sheet together and walk around the classroom. "I'm the head and you're the legs", Aymeline tells Mariam. Alex asks if she can join them. "Ok you can be the hump. You be in the middle". Alex joins them and says, "We need to get camel food!" Aymeline says, "Yeah let's look outside!"*

You might think that is a rather short story but it has many of the features of the stories that humans all over the world tell each other. The third-person narrator tells us about a relationship where one person suggests a course of action to another. Someone else gets involved and they become three. The threesome has adventures – we do not know what they might be because we do not know what happens next, but plans have been made.

Here is another story:

> *Jacob, you were playing in the sandpit, you were using a watering can to pour water down a pipe into the sand pit. You said, "Look, I made a super flood. I need to try it from the other side". You found a piece of pipe. Then you poured water down the pipe and watched it flow into the second pipe. You had to readjust the position of the guttering a few times until the water flowed straight into it. Then you found a piece of guttering and added that onto the pipe and tested whether*

the water would flow into the guttering as well. It did and you were pleased, saying, "Look, look". Next you found a piece of pipe and put this at the end of the guttering leaning up against the edge of the sand pit. Then you poured the water down the pipe and watched it flow along the pipe, gutter and then up the pipe leaning against the side of the sand pit. We both watched it flow back down again. Then you collected some sand and put it in the guttering – I asked you what you thought might happen, you told me, "It will block the water, maybe make another flood". You watched the water flowing down and saw it backing up behind the sand and flowing over. You let other children help with putting water down the pipes.

It is not just the length that makes this a different sort of story from the first one. Here the narrator is recalling and describing the actions of the child, the main protagonist, not to an unseen audience but to the child himself.

You can find both these stories on the East London Early Years and Schools Partnership website (2017) at www.eleysp.co.uk/celebrating-childrens-learning/.

These sorts of assessments based on observations mean that young children's learning is identified and recorded as part of an ongoing process. They identify what children can do and help practitioners to plan new learning experiences.

Narrative or story is a very important element of effective early years assessment. Early years policy makers sometimes fail to recognise that assessment is different from testing and measurement. It is important to distinguish between assessment for learning and assessment for accountability. No one instrument can be fit for both purposes. Assessment for learning is ongoing and informs the teaching and learning process. It extends children's learning because it enhances teaching and tells each child's individual learning story. All other forms of assessment, including baseline assessment, serve as checks on whether or not learning has occurred, not as a means – in themselves – of bringing about learning. Driven by management and accountability, these kinds of assessments elevate scores over narrative accounts of children's learning, in a format that can allow the 'value added' by the school to be calculated.

In this chapter, we are going to draw on these two stories from the Celebrating Children's Learning webpage to explore the ways in which children's engagement, motivation and thinking can be observed and assessed in effective early years pedagogy. We will also consider the growing evidence that children's experiences in the early years lay the foundations for how they learn, with far-reaching effects through their school years and beyond. Rather than observation and reflection on *how* children learn being an afterthought in our assessment practice, we need first and foremost to celebrate and support children as learners through the Characteristics of Effective Learning.

Start with observing

The practitioners who recorded Jacob and Aymeline's experiences clearly observed the children's actions carefully. These are a far cry from the sort of 'empty' observations too often found in portfolios alongside a photo, such as 'Jacob really enjoyed playing with the water and pipes' or 'Aymeline used her imagination in playing with the fabric'. These are rich observations that reflect the four key features of best practice outlined in the Celebrating Children's Learning project:

- *You can 'hear' the child's voice or 'get a feel' for their play* – We almost feel we are there, hearing Jacob and Aymeline's own thoughts and following their play.
- *There is keen observation of the child's exploration, play and thinking* – It is a detailed account of their actions, including glimpses of their thinking through what they say.
- *The practitioner has noticed that the child is learning a new skill, or is making new links between aspects of knowledge* – They are building on their ideas of camels and floods, making predictions and representing what they know.
- *There are examples of sustained shared thinking, or a response from the child showing their feeling of awe and wonder* – We can see their learning: Jacob is aware of his ability to test his ideas, is excited about his discoveries, and discusses his predictions, while Aymeline and her friends spark off each other's ideas.

Such lively pictures of play provide a window into understanding something about each child's interests and learning. But an observation is only the start of the central cycle in effective early years practice: observe, assess, plan, act – and then observe the child's response and start round the cycle again. Observation and assessment is useful only if it helps us to be more accurate educators, better matching our interactions and provision to the child's needs in order to support and enhance learning. This observation, assessment and planning cycle in the Early Years Foundation Stage (EYFS) is represented in Figure 2.1, which encapsulates the main aspects of the job done by early years practitioners in supporting children's progress through the EYFS.

What do we make of detailed observations like these? Practitioners eager to identify learning often keep in mind the seven EYFS areas of learning and development. They might, for example, consider what Jacob

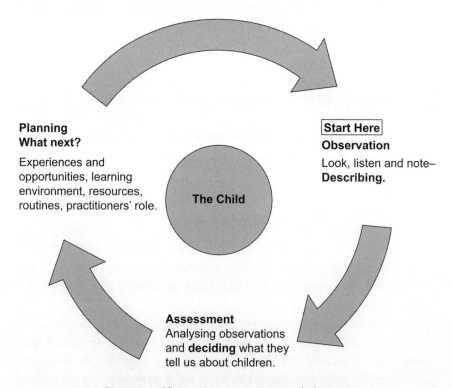

Planning
What next?

Experiences and opportunities, learning environment, resources, routines, practitioners' role.

The Child

Start Here
Observation

Look, listen and note–
Describing.

Assessment
Analysing observations and **deciding** what they tell us about children.

Figure 2.1 Observation, assessment and planning

Source: Early Education (2012) *Development Matters in the Early Years Foundation Stage*, London: Early Education, Crown copyright. [Online] Available at www.early-education.org.uk and for download at www.early-education.org.uk/development-matters-early-years-foundation-stage-eyfs (Last accessed 31 July 2017)

has shown us and assume he knows about the action of sand and water or about floods in the wider world (Understanding the World), or consider how he handles the large equipment (Physical Development), how he expresses himself (Communication and Language), or how he shares his experience with his peers (Personal, Social and Emotional Development). But this analysis might miss the first and critically important part of Jacob's learning story. Without the learning behaviours and attitudes Jacob employs to drive his actions – described in the EYFS framework as the Characteristics of Effective Learning – he would be standing still in his learning and development.

The observation-assessment-planning cycle must be seen, however, in the context of the broader EYFS. A Unique Child, Positive Relationships, Enabling Environments and Learning and Development are the four themes of the EYFS and are interrelated:

> **A Unique Child** actively drives their own learning, reaching out and making sense of their experiences with people and world around them. Within warm and loving **Positive Relationships** the child experiences emotional safety which is the bedrock to learning about how to be a person, and joins the world of learning with and from others. **Enabling Environments** provide the stimulating outdoor and indoor experiences – in settings and at home – which challenge children, respond to their interests and meet their needs. The result of these three elements interacting together is the child's **Learning and Development.**
>
> (Moylett and Stewart, 2012, p. 6)

Our habits of mind are formed as our brains and bodies develop and we come to understand ourselves as learners. The role of adults in this process is key. When young children are left to their own devices in a stimulating learning environment, most will learn through playing and exploring – but this is not enough. It is through the active intervention, guidance and support of a skilled adult that children make the most progress in their learning. This does not mean pushing children too far or too fast, but instead meeting children where they are emotionally and intellectually. It means being a partner with children, enjoying with them the power of their curiosity and the 'thrill, will and skill' of finding out what they can do.

The 'thrill, will and skill' represent the characteristics of effective early learning:

- Playing and exploring – the *thrill* of discovery
- Active learning – the *will* to keep going
- Creating and thinking critically – the *skill* of developing ideas

An acknowledgement of the importance of what we now know about self-regulation lies at the heart of the emphasis on the Characteristics of Effective Learning in the EYFS. As well as managing feelings and behaviour, self-regulation involves attitudes and dispositions for learning and an ability to be aware of one's own thinking.

Importance of relationships and well-being

Every few seconds, another human is born into the world. How long each baby survives and whether they lead happy lives between birth and death will depend on many factors, including how they are loved and cared for in their early years. The fact that well-being underpins learning has been known for many years, but developments in neuroscience have confirmed that early attachment relationships are crucial for brain development (Gerhardt, 2004; Conkbayir, 2017). Warm, positive interactions and exploring the world with the senses build a brain that can trust and care for others, manage emotions, and learn effectively. Our prime caregivers help us to regulate our emotions by being consistently responsive and sensitive to our needs. As babies, we need and seek constant repetition of acts of being loved, trusted and given control to begin to understand ourselves and others. The most fundamental task of a baby is to learn how to meet her needs. When her signals are recognised and she receives what is often referred to as a 'contingent' response based on what she actually needs, rather than on what the carer thinks she might or should need, she will calm, feel secure and begin to be able to regulate her own behaviour.

These repeated positive experiences help us to build up patterns of response and habits of mind – the strong connections that will remain for life. When babies work out that they can depend on and trust a caregiver (usually, but not always, their mother) who is consistently responsive and sensitive to their physical and emotional needs, they have what is called a 'secure attachment'.

Babies can also form close bonds with a small group of other people who know them well. These relationships are vital to their learning and development and explain why the key person role in settings is so important.

Secure attachment supports us to be effective learners as well as happier, healthier people and this has been recognised in various government commissioned reports (Field, 2010; Marmot, 2010; Allen, 2011) that argue for more investment in early years. An important way in which attachment supports us to be good learners is that it gives us a secure base from which to explore the world. It supports our self-confidence and our ability to relate to others and it enables us to try new things and take risks. It also supports our resilience in the face of setbacks; whatever goes wrong, we know that attachment figure will be there to support us.

The International Resilience Project surveyed parents, caregivers and 589 children from 14 countries to find out what supported resilience. Grotberg (1995) reported that there appeared to be three main sources of resilience: I have, I am and I can.

I have

- People around me I trust and who love me, no matter what
- People who set limits for me so I know when to stop before there is danger or trouble
- People who show me how to do things right by the way they do things
- People who want me to learn to do things on my own
- People who help me when I am sick, in danger or need to learn

I am

- A person people can like and love
- Glad to do nice things for others and show my concern
- Respectful of myself and others
- Willing to be responsible for what I do
- Sure things will be all right

I can

- Talk to others about things that frighten me or bother me
- Find ways to solve problems that I face

- Control myself when I feel like doing something not right or dangerous
- Figure out when it is a good time to talk to someone or to take action
- Find someone to help me when I need it

Resilience results from a combination of these features. As Grotberg explains:

> A resilient child does not need all of these features to be resilient, but one is not enough. A child may be loved (I HAVE), but if he or she has no inner strength (I AM) or social, interpersonal skills (I CAN), there can be no resilience. A child may have a great deal of self-esteem (I AM), but if he or she does not know how to communicate with others or solve problems (I CAN), and has no one to help him or her (I HAVE), the child is not resilient. A child may be very verbal and speak well (I CAN), but if he or she has no empathy (I AM) or does not learn from role models (I HAVE), there is no resilience.
>
> (Grotberg, 1995, p. 10)

Grotberg's features of resilience contain messages for the roles of parents and practitioners. Adults who promote resilience encourage children to become increasingly autonomous, independent and responsible, and to approach people and situations positively. They become regulatory partners teaching children how to communicate with others, solve problems, and successfully regulate negative thoughts, feelings and behaviours. These skills and dispositions are contained within the EYFS prime areas and the Characteristics of Effective Learning and support us to become strong people and effective learners.

Being involved is one of the five domains of learning disposition described by Carr (2001). She describes dispositions as a combination of motivation and learning strategies. They are an integral part of the 'Learning Story' approach to observation, assessment and planning developed in New Zealand and are related to the strands of the New Zealand early years curriculum, Te Whariki. All the strands of Te Whariki are interwoven but it is significant that being involved is particularly related to the well-being strand; involvement is what practitioners look for when children are feeling a sense of well-being.

This combination of well-being and involvement as an important indicator of children's learning has also been developed by Ferre Laevers at Leuven University in Belgium and extensively used by Pascal et al. (2001) in the UK as part of the Effective Early Learning (EEL) and Baby EEL (BEEL) programmes. Laevers (2000) explains why, if we truly want to assess how children are developing and learning, we should consider these two import-ant aspects, balancing emotional and cognitive aspects of how and why children learn.

> [W]e first have to explore the degree in which children do feel at ease, act spontaneously, show vitality and self-confidence. All this indicates that their emotional well-being is o.k. and that their physical needs, the need for tenderness and affection, the need for safety and clarity, the need for social recognition, the need to feel competent and the need for meaning in life and moral value are satisfied.
>
> The second criterion – involvement – is linked to the developmen-tal process and urges the adult to set up a challenging environment favouring concentrated, intrinsically motivated activity. Care settings and schools have to succeed on both tasks: only paying attention to emotional wellbeing and a positive climate is not enough, while efforts to enhance involvement will only have an impact if children and students feel at home and are free from emotional constraints.

The next section looks in more detail at the cognitive side of this balance. Then we return to the implications for effective pedagogy, including assess-ment practice, which supports children's learning.

How children learn

Alongside emotional well-being and emotional self-regulation, which underpin children's readiness to learn, there are cognitive factors that deter-mine how children take in information from the world around them, apply their energy and focus on their activities, and form ideas to make sense of their experiences of the world and people around them.

The cognitive factors in young children's learning are described in the Characteristics of Effective Learning. These were introduced into the EYFS statutory framework in 2012, building on the 2008 non-statutory guidance that described the process of learning and development through play and exploration, active learning, and creativity and critical thinking. Paying attention to the Characteristics is currently a legal requirement in EYFS prac-tice, with the statutory framework stating that:

In planning and guiding children's activities, practitioners must reflect on the different ways that children learn and reflect these in their practice. Three characteristics of effective teaching and learning are:

- Playing and exploring – children investigate and experience things, and 'have a go'
- Active learning – children concentrate and keep on trying if they encounter difficulties, and enjoy achievements
- Creating and thinking critically – children have and develop their own ideas, make links between ideas, and develop strategies for doing things

(DfE, 2017)

The Characteristics were introduced into the statutory framework in order to heighten attention to children's agency as learners, covering elements such as engagement, attitudes to learning, self-regulation, motivation, perseverance, creativity, problem-solving and metacognition. Recent research sheds light on all of these areas, and on the role of adults in their development.

Educators often identify objectives or 'next steps' for children based on their assessment of *what* children know, understand and can do within the curricular areas – and there is evidence that when early years programmes focus on specific content in areas such as literacy or mathematics, children can make rapid progress in these areas. Research demonstrates, however, that such early gains may be of short-lived benefit.

An approach that may pay better dividends in the end is to concentrate more on *how* the children are learning. A steadily growing body of evidence bears out the importance of seeing the EYFS as truly foundational in developing children's learning powers, and it is now well established in research and practice that a major determinant of children's success as learners is their ability to self-regulate (Whitebread et al., 2005; Bronson, 2000; Pasternak and Whitebread, 2010; Whitebread and Basilio, 2012). A meta-analysis of outcomes of early childhood education approaches found that 'the short-term effects of more academic programmes wore off after a few years in primary school', while with programmes based on 'cognitive-developmental approaches emphasising children's choice, autonomy and self-regulation . . . longitudinal effects on educational and social adjustment outcomes were found' (Chambers et al., 2010).

Research: playing and exploring

The drive to play and explore can be understood as growing from the inborn need to develop competence as described in self-determination theory (Deci and Ryan, 2000). A growth mindset leads to ongoing engagement with challenge, and confidence to learn from mistakes; this drive can be undermined by a fixed mindset, characterised by the belief that abilities are set so there is no use trying to do challenging things, with fear of failure arising from the desire to avoid looking incompetent (Dweck, 2006).

Most early years practitioners readily say that they believe in 'learning through play', but play is a complex process and means different things to different people. This definition emphasises the child's control:

> Play is freely chosen by the child, and is under the control of the child. The child decides how to play, how long to sustain the play, what the play is about, and who to play with. There are many forms of play, but it is usually highly creative, open-ended and imaginative. It requires active engagement of the players, and can be deeply satisfying (DCSF, 2009).

Such child-directed play is a strong venue for the development of effective learning behaviours. Studies have shown that children's explorations and problem-solving are enhanced through play and playful pedagogy employed by adults. In one study, children were less likely to explore and discover novel information when a function of a toy was presented through direct instruction (Bonawitza et al., 2011). In another study, children were shown a novel toy, either a ball with rubbery protuberances or a stuffed toy with rings and tabs attached. Both of these could be rolled, squished, knocked, pulled, stretched, shaken and so on, with a certain sequence of actions resulting in a musical effect. In some cases, the researchers demonstrated the toy, while in others, the adult pretended to explore to try to find out how to make the musical result. The researchers found that when children had been shown an exploratory, playful approach to the toy, they later found new and effective solutions to the problem, but when it had been demonstrated to them, they restricted their explorations and were less likely to find effective solutions (Buchsbaum et al., 2011).

Children talk as they play, both to themselves and to others, and this 'thinking aloud' has a strong impact on their developing self-regulation. When children use private speech, talking to themselves to narrate what they are doing, they are providing their own 'scaffolding', guiding and controlling their own behaviour and thinking. At times of greatest concentration and challenge, they will often talk themselves through a sequence of actions: 'This has to go in the hole. Hmm, it's very tricky. Push it hard. There!' Self-talk includes children working through ideas, surmounting obstacles, mastering cognitive or social skills, or managing intense emotion (Berk and Spuhl, 1995). The more children use self-talk in play, the more it supports them to internalise control. Young children who make self-guiding comments while working on challenging tasks are more attentive and involved and perform better than their less talkative peers (Winsler, 1997). Children aged four and five who were judged by their preschool teachers to be good at regulating emotion used more private speech during free play, art and puzzle activities than did classmates who were rated as poorly regulated (Broderick, 2001).

Imaginative play, and especially dramatic play with others, brings even greater gains in self-regulation, as children need to negotiate roles and activities in order to keep the play going. Gains in self-regulation through sociodramatic play can be especially strong for highly impulsive children, who benefit greatly from adult support that is sensitive to children's ideas. Studies of children with weak play skills who receive adult encouragement to engage in make-believe, compared to other activities or no play, show gains in imaginativeness of play content, mental test scores, impulse control, coherence of storytelling, and capacity to empathise with others (Whitebread and O'Sullivan, 2012). Children who are stuck in violent play themes may need more adult support to develop greater attention, development of narrative, use of language and perspective-taking in play (Dunn and Hughes, 2001).

Research: active learning

'Active learning' describes the child actively driving their own learning, with strong motivation, focus, persistence, and bouncing back from difficulties. Whether children persist with challenge at age four is a stronger predictor of educational success than reading scores (McClelland et al., 2013). Differences in concentration and persistence are apparent by age two, and link to parenting styles; children are more persistent when parents sensitively support babies' autonomy in their activities, responding to their child's attempts rather than attempting to control them (Grolnick, Bridges and Frodi, 1984).

Intrinsic motivation – when the motivation comes from within and the activity is satisfying for its own sake, rather than for external reward – is associated with high-quality learning, as learners are more involved, develop deeper understanding, use strategies more effectively, apply understanding in new situations, have more enjoyment, gain greater knowledge and are more persistent than when they are extrinsically motivated (Lepper, Corpus and Iyengar, 2005).

Stickers and other rewards are tangible extrinsic motivators that can undermine intrinsic motivation (Ryan and Deci, 2000). More subtly, praise is a verbal reward that could be considered in the light of intrinsic/extrinsic motivation, as it can become an extrinsic motivator if it labels the person (fostering fixed mindset) rather than giving precise feedback on the processes or products, and if it is perceived as controlling by the child. Excessive praise can be especially limiting for children with low self-esteem who become further afraid of failure (Deci and Ryan, 2000; Dweck, 2006; Brummelman et al., 2014).

Intrinsic motivation is fostered when tasks are aligned to learners' interests, involve choice, offer an optimal level of challenge and are open-ended – in other words, in play and playful adult-led experiences (Lai, 2011).

Research: creating and thinking critically

Children's creativity involves discovery for themselves – coming up with ideas and ways of expressing them that are new to the child. This is facilitated by adults using an informal, open approach (Kudryavtsev, 2011).

Imagination is central to children's developing ability to think about abstract ideas and to make links in their experience. Presenting problems to children in a fantasy mode, calling on their imagination or pretending, helps children to reason successfully to solve logical problems. They are able to suspend their dependence on more limited experience and hold ideas in mind in order to make logical connections (Amsel, Trionfi and Campbell, 2005; Da Graça et al., 2005).

Goswami (2015) has reviewed evidence of how children learn, and concludes that children possess and demonstrate all the main types of learning (statistical learning, learning by imitation, learning by analogy and causal learning) even as babies. She points out that:

Children think and reason largely in the same ways as adults. However, they lack experience, and they are still developing important

> metacognitive and executive function skills. Learning in classrooms can be enhanced if children are given diverse experiences and are helped to develop self-reflective and self-regulatory skills via teacher modelling, conversation and guidance around social situations like play, sharing and conflict resolutions.
>
> (Goswami, 2015, p. 25)

Critical thinking involves developing metacognition, which means being aware of controlling your own thinking and learning – choosing strategies, checking and adapting approaches as needed. Whitebread et al. (2007) found extensive evidence of metacognitive behaviours within the three- to five-year age range that occurred most frequently during learning activities that were initiated by the children, involved them working in pairs or small groups unsupervised by adults, and involved extensive collaboration and talk (that is, learning contexts that might be characterized as peer-assisted learning). Children working in unsupervised small groups showed more evidence of metacognitive monitoring and control, compared to working individually or in groups with adult support.

An important message for practitioners is that metacognitive and self-regulatory abilities, under-pinned by efficient executive functioning, have a major impact on children's general and academic development – and that how adults support these areas can have significant influence on how they develop (Whitebread and O'Sullivan, 2012).

Executive function is the 'command and control' centre in the mind, dealing with the constant onslaught of perceptions and thoughts. It is described as having three main elements: working memory, inhibition control and mental flexibility. Executive control, based in the frontal cerebral cortex of the brain, develops throughout childhood and does not reach maturity until late adolescence. Rather than understanding these as something that must be left to develop at their own pace, however, recent neuroscience research shows that they are connected with multi-sensory networks of neurons distributed across the entire brain. According to a recent research review, 'It is suggested that the brain's capacity to organise this skill set to filter distractions, prioritize tasks, set and achieve goals, and control impulses, lies at the heart of all learning' (BERA-TACTYC, 2017).

Why children learn

When we observe children and reflect on what we have noticed, the central question in our mind must be 'What can I understand about this child?'

Recognising the unique nature of each child requires approaching our reflections with openness, not an expectation that the child will be reaching for the next predictable milestone. So we take our attention off a set of curricular targets, and put it onto the child's own story. We wonder about their interests, questions, motivations, feelings and thoughts. Only when we have considered what the experience means to the child can we begin to plan how we can be a supportive and stimulating partner in their learning.

Children do not learn because they are keen to progress through a curriculum framework, and we hope they are intrinsically motivated and not just trying to please us. We need to recognise that the child has their own drive to learn and their own agenda, and that building and maintaining that drive is what will help them to flourish in the face of the unknown challenges their future might bring.

Self-determination theory describes three inborn human drives: to become competent, to have autonomy, and to relate to others. We feel satisfied when we push ourselves to achieve something that makes us feel increasingly competent in the world we live in. Those efforts are supported by the drive to make autonomous decisions and make things happen for ourselves. And we have a social drive to belong and participate with others.

Children's internal drives lead to the learning behaviours described in the Characteristics of Effective Learning. Through those ways of acting with objects and other people, they dive into experiences and achieve strong learning outcomes. We can truly celebrate that children are powerful learners.

Strong learners

Let us go back to the learning stories at the beginning of this chapter and think about how Aymeline and Jacob were demonstrating the Characteristics of Effective Learning in action. We start with playing and exploring – the ways in which children engage with learning.

Playing and exploring – engagement

Finding out and exploring

- Showing curiosity about objects, events and people
- Using senses to explore the world around them

- Engaging in open-ended activity
- Showing particular interests

Playing with what they know

- Pretending objects are things from their experience
- Representing their experiences in play
- Taking on a role in their play
- Acting out experiences with other people

Being willing to 'have a go'

- Initiating activities
- Seeking challenge
- Showing a 'can do' attitude
- Taking a risk, engaging in new experiences, and learning from failures

We can see all three strands of playing and exploring in action in Ayme-line's story. Aymeline takes the lead in this play. She is curious about camels and wants to explore this particular interest. She and Mariam are skilled in using the fabric in pretend play to represent a camel and take on the role of the camel themselves. They are willing to 'have a go' and are happy for Alex to join them and welcome her suggestion, which all three act on, continuing the play outside. As well as the aspects of playing and exploring, here we can also make some assessment of the three children's social skills. They appear to understand that sometimes one person leads play but others can contribute. They know how to keep pretend play going and are highly motivated.

High levels of motivation are displayed by Jacob in his exploration of the pipes, guttering, water and sand. Consider how active he is in his learning.

Active learning – motivation

Being involved and concentrating

- Maintaining focus on their activity for a period of time
- Showing high levels of energy, fascination

- Not easily distracted
- Paying attention to details

Keeping on trying

- Persisting with activity when challenges occur
- Showing a belief that more effort or a different approach will pay off
- Bouncing back after difficulties

Enjoying achieving what they set out to do

- Showing satisfaction in meeting their own goals
- Being proud of how they accomplished something – not just the end result
- Enjoying meeting challenges for their own sake rather than external rewards or praise

We can see that he is deeply involved with high levels of energy and fascination. He pays attention to detail and persists with solving the problem of getting the water flowing as he wants it to. The practitioner notes that he is pleased with the result and he is clearly enjoying meeting this self-generated challenge for its own sake. Although he is keen for the practitioner to look, he is not asking for praise or a sticker – he is sharing his pride in his own achievement.

Jacob is also demonstrating his ability to create and think critically.

Creating and thinking critically – thinking

Having their own ideas

- Thinking of ideas
- Finding ways to solve problems
- Finding new ways to do things

Making links

- Making links and noticing patterns in their experience
- Making predictions

- Testing their ideas
- Developing ideas of grouping, sequences, cause and effect

Choosing ways to do things

- Planning, making decisions about how to approach a task, solve a problem and reach a goal
- Monitoring how well their activities are going
- Changing strategy as needed
- Reviewing how well the approach worked

Jacob announces that he has made a 'super flood'. This is his own idea and he wants to extend his learning by trying it 'from the other side'. The practitioner pays close attention as he finds new ways to do things, makes links with previous experience, predicts what will happen and tests his ideas, monitoring how well different approaches work and changing strategy as needed. He is being both a creative and critical thinker. The practitioner has seen his learning power in action because she is not focusing on the areas of learning but on the child and his learning story.

Jacob's story is told by the practitioner. It is designed to be a tool for sustained shared thinking in that he can review his own learning process thanks to the very detailed account of it provided. She is talking on paper about what Jacob planned to do, what he did and what worked well. Having that conversation with Jacob himself, possibly illustrated with photographs, could be an important next step in taking his thinking forward.

Paying attention to how children are learning is the key to successful pedagogy in the early years. Paying attention does not mean ticking a list of *Development Matters* statements, writing lots of post-it notes, or ensuring the e-tracker tells you where the child is. It means the sort of attention that tunes into the child, which is fascinated by their processes and able to analyse their learning power. As Kline (1999, p. 36) so rightly claims: 'The quality of your attention determines the quality of other people's thinking'.

Pedagogy

All practitioners observe children, but if we are not open to what they are telling us we may miss what their stories say about their engagement, motivation and thinking. If we spend all our time providing adult-led focused activities we may become so bogged down in 'learning intentions' that we miss the actual learning that is going on.

Stevens (2014, p. 95) illustrates this brilliantly:

> We may be so busy 'observing' how children are ordering numbers from zero to ten, as they peg number cards they have made, onto a washing line, as part of an adult planned experience that we fail to observe how they are approaching the process. So we may miss:

Flavia: Piling the number cards up, then collecting another set from the maths learning zone and matching the numerals – put a '2' with a '2' and a '3' with a '3'. Then shuffling all the cards and dealing them out to friends.

Serge: Sorting the cards into piles of 'even' and 'odd' numbers – counting in twos out loud. Walking away, still chanting 'two, four, six, eight, who do we appreciate?'

Charlotte: Singing 'Ten in a Bed' as she fixes the cards to the line, and calling to Charlene "come and play 10 in a bed with me, bring the babies". Spending over twenty minutes pegging up the cards, laying them in a row and matching one toy to each, singing and laughing.

Rifat: Struggling with using the pegs to fix the cards onto the washing line. Looking hard at the pegs, practising open and closing them with two hands, and watching other children. Then having another go and beaming as the card remains fixed to the line.

Milo: Refusing to join in with the activity when invited by the practitioner, but later returning, when the adult and group of children leaves. Looking at the cards, and fixing the '4' card onto the line – between the '7' and '8', saying "Four, I four".

As Stevens says, it would be easy for a practitioner to miss some of the non-mathematical learning being demonstrated here, such as Rifat's physical development.

Stevens (2014, p. 96) goes on to explore the aspects of the Characteristics of Effective Learning that might be missed through this concentration on a narrow focus.

Flavia: The way that Flavia is thinking and learning – **'having her own ideas'** about how to use the resource and putting them into practice **(Creating and thinking critically)**

Serge: The way Serge is thinking and **'making links'** in his learning – how he is thinking about the oral 'counting in twos' activity earlier in the week **(Creating and thinking critically)**

Charlotte: The way Charlotte continues to be **motivated** by a task she sets herself – how she is **'involved and concentrating'** for a prolonged period **(Active Learning)**

Rifat: The way Rifat exhibits his **motivation** – how he **'keeps on trying'** and **'enjoys achieving what he sets out to do' (Active Learning)**

Milo: The way Milo becomes **engaged** in the experience, after initial reluctance – being willing to **'have a go'** away from the group **(Playing and Exploring)**

Noticing the ways in which children are engaging, how they are motivated, and what they might be thinking about is the most effective way to support them across all areas of the curriculum. Early years teaching is not a transmission process, feeding knowledge into children's minds with children as passive receivers. Children must do the learning work, and the educator's role is to work with the process of learning itself.

Whenever we make an assessment based on observation, it is our best informed guess – we make a judgment about how the child feels, what the child is curious about, is excited or puzzled by, or is trying to do. The most powerful use of observation and assessment is when we plan in that moment how best we could respond. We might decide to enter in the activity, mirroring the child's actions in order to lead to conversation that helps both parties to think together. We might provide a small piece of relevant information, or encourage thinking about strategies and what works. We might decide to introduce another resource that would support what we think the child is trying to do, or might challenge them to take their efforts and thinking further. When the practitioner asks Jacob what he thinks might happen, she is wondering with him as well as getting him to articulate his own thinking and speculate that there might be another flood.

Close observation and reflection about children's learning processes will also enable us to step back from the moment to plan our practice and provision to support children's development as learners. Have we provided an environment, routines, activities and adult interaction that allow children to exercise choice, autonomy, use their imaginations, and think for themselves? Are there particular children who need us to support their purposeful focus, or to take a risk in new situations? Do we provide regular opportunities for children to review their activities, talking about their strategies and their own thoughts about what they have learned?

There are no 'right' answers to what the next steps should be for practitioners who strive to provide excellent support for learning. Understanding what is in children's minds, where they are leading us, and how best to respond requires adults to be curious, motivated, creative and thoughtful – and monitor to adjust strategies as needed because we will not always get it right. This is why these are truly characteristics of effective teaching, as well as learning. In an ongoing process, we need to tune in, be alert to the drivers of children's learning, and seek to understand what the children are showing us.

It is never as straightforward as matching a single item on a tracker to a 'next step'. Children are forging their own learning paths through unknown territory, and the story of that journey cannot be broken up piecemeal. We cannot understand a story by considering a single word, sentence or paragraph pulled out at random – we would literally lose the plot. In the same way, everything we observe about children must be considered in the light of the whole: where have the child's interests, questions, ways of approaching the world come from, where are they headed, and why? Just as a story is driven forward by a central plot, children's learning is driven forward by their own forces that deserve our focus as the centre of the story.

Neither of the stories explored here are neat and tidy. They are not in the 'Once upon a time to happily ever after' mode because they are both part of individual children's learning and life stories, woven in the present from the past and peering into a future they, and we, do not yet know. As long ago as 1964, John Holt claimed that it was foolish to keep on trying to fill children up with knowledge and that instead we should be trying to give children the skills to love the challenges of learning, so they will be able to learn anything they need in future. If our assessment of children's learning focuses on their engagement, motivation and thinking and we are prepared to support and challenge them as they move forward, they will be those wonderful lifelong learners who think deeply, act wisely and believe in their own and others' capacities to make a difference.

There are lots of things that may take our attention away from children's stories, but that will not stop them unfolding. As Magnavacchi and Wilenski

(2015, p. 65) remind us, 'When we decide to focus on children's storying it is like tuning in to a radio station that has always been broadcasting. The children's stories don't begin because we are listening, but we hear them more clearly and in finer detail'.

Let us find time to listen and think together!

References

Allen, G. (2011) *Early Intervention: The Next Steps. An Independent Report to Her Majesty's Government.* London: Cabinet Office, Crown Copyright.

Amsel, E., Trionfi, G. and Campbell, R. (2005) Reasoning about make-believe and hypothetical suppositions: Towards a theory of belief-contravening reasoning. *Cognitive Development,* 20 (4), October–December, 545–575.

BERA-TACTYC (2017) *Early Childhood Research Review 2001–2017.* London: British Educational Research Association Early Childhood Special Interest Group and TACTYC: Association for Professional Development in Early Years, p. 72.

Berk, L. E. and Spuhl, S. T. (1995) Maternal interaction, private speech, and task performance in preschool children. *Early Childhood Research Quarterly,* 10, 145–169.

Bonawitza, E., Shaftob, P., Gweonc, H., Goodmand, N. D., Spelkee, E. and Schulzc, L. (2011) The double-edged sword of pedagogy: Instruction limits spontaneous exploration and discovery. *Cognition,* 120 (3), September, 322–330.

Broderick, N. Y. (2001) An investigation of the relationship between private speech and emotion regulation in preschool-age children. *Dissertation Abstracts International: Section B the sciences and engineering,* 61 (11B), 6125.

Bronson, M. (2000). *Self-Regulation in Early Childhood: Nature and Nurture.* New York: The Guilford Press.

Brummelman, E., Thomaes, S., Overbeek, G., de Castro, O. B., den Hout, V. and van den Hout, M. A. (2014) On feeding those hungry for praise: Person praise backfires in children with low self-esteem. *Journal of Experimental Psychology: General,* 143 (1), February, 9–14.

Buchsbaum, D., Gopnik, A., Griffiths, T. L. and Shaftob, P. (2011) Probabilistic models of cognitive development: Children's imitation of causal action sequences is influenced by statistical and pedagogical evidence. *Cognition,* 120 (3), September, 331–340.

Carr, M. (2001) Te Whariki curriculum and assessment guidance. In *Assessment in Early Childhood Settings: Learning Stories.* London: Sage.

Chambers, B., Cheung, A., Slavin, R. E., Smith, D. and Laurenzano, M. (2010) *Effective Early Childhood Education Programmes: A Best-Evidence Synthesis.* Center for Research and Reform in Education. http://eric.ed.gov/?id=ED527643

Conkbayir, M. (2017) *Early Childhood and Neuroscience.* London: Bloomsbury.

Da Graça, B. B., Dias, M., Roazzi, A., O'Brien, D. and Harris, P. (2005) Logical reasoning and fantasy contexts: Eliminating differences between children with and without experience in school. *Inter-American Journal of Psychology – 2005*, 39 (1), 13–22.

DCSF (2009) *00775–2009BKT-EN, Learning, Playing and Interacting: Good Practice in the Early Years Foundation Stage*. Nottingham, UK: DCSF Publications.

Deci, E. L. and Ryan, R. M. (2000) The "what" and "why" of goal pursuits: Human needs and the self-determination of behavior. *Psychological Inquiry*, 11, 227–268.

DfE (2017), DFE-00169–2017, *Statutory Framework for the Early Years Foundation Stage: Setting the Standards for Learning, Development and Care for Children From Birth to Five, 1.9*. Nottingham, UK: DCSF Publications.

Dunn, J. and Hughes, C. (2001) "I got some swords and you're dead!": Violent fantasy, antisocial behavior, friendship, and moral sensibility in young children. *Child Development,* 72 (2), 491–505.

Dweck, C. (2006) *Mindset: The New Psychology of Success*. New York, NY: Ballantyne Books.

Early Education (2012) *Development Matters in the Early Years Foundation Stage*. London: Early Education, Crown copyright (Online). www.early-education.org. uk (Last accessed 31 July 2017)

Field, F. (2010) *The Foundation Years: Preventing Poor Children Becoming Poor Adults*. The report of the Independent Review on Poverty and Life Chances. London: Cabinet Office, Crown copyright.

Gerhardt, S. (2004) *Why Love Matters: How Affection Shapes a Baby's Brain*. London: Routledge.

Goswami, U. (2015) *Children's Cognitive Development and Learning*. CPRT Research Survey 3. New York: Cambridge Primary Review Trust. ISBN 978-0-9931032-2-3.

Grolnick, W., Bridges, L. and Frodi, A. (1984) Maternal control style and the mastery motivation of one-year-olds. *Infant Mental Health Journal*, 5, 72–82.

Grotberg, E. (1995) *A Guide to Promoting Resilience in Children: Strengthening the Human Spirit*. The Hague: Bernard Van Leer Foundation.

Holt, J. (1964) *How Children Fail*. New York, NY: Pitman Publishing Corp.

Kline, N. (1999) *Time to Think, Listening to Ignite the Human Mind*. London: Ward Lock.

Krafft, K. C. and Berk, L. E. (1998) Private speech in two preschools: Significance of open-ended activities and make-believe play for verbal regulation. *Early Childhood Research Quarterly*, 13, 637–658.

Kudryavtsev, V. T. (2011): The phenomenon of child creativity. *International Journal of Early Years Education*, 19 (1), 45–53.

Laevers, F. (2000) Forward to basics! Deep-level learning and the experiential approach. *Early Years*, 20 (2), 20–29.

Lai, E. R. (2011) *Motivation: A Literature Review*. Research Report, Pearson. http:// images.pearsonassessments.com/images/tmrs/Motivation_Review_final.pdf (Last accessed 31 July 2017)

Lepper, M. R., Corpus, H. J. and Iyengar, S. (2005) Intrinsic and extrinsic motivational orientations in the classroom: Age differences and academic correlates. *Journal of Educational Psychology Copyright 2005 by the American Psychological Association*, 97 (2), 184–196.

Magnavacchi, L. and Wilenski, D. (2015) *The Revolutionary Baby*. Worthing: On Reflection Publishing.

Marmot, M. (2010) *Fair Society, Healthy Lives: Equity From the Start*. London: UCL, Institute of Health Equity.

McClelland, M. M., Acock, A. C., Piccinin, A., Rhea, S. A. and Stallings, M. C. (2013) Relations between preschool attention Span-persistence and age 25 educational outcomes. *Early Childhood Research Quarterly*, 28 (2), 314–324.

Moylett, H. and Stewart, N. (2012) *Understanding the Revised Early Years Foundation Stage*. London: Early Education.

Pascal, C., Bertram, A., Ramsden, F. and Saunders, M. (2001) *Effective Early Learning Programme (EEL)* (3rd ed.). Worcester, UK: University College Worcester, Centre for Research in Early Childhood Education.

Pasternak, P. and Whitebread, D. (2010) The role of parenting in children's self-regulated learning. *Educational Research Review*, 5, 220–242.

Ryan, R. M. and Deci, E. L. (2000) Intrinsic and extrinsic motivations: classic definitions and new directions. *Contemporary Educational Psychology*, 25, 54–67 doi:10.1006/ceps.1999.1020 (Online) www.idealibrary.com

Stevens, J. (2014) Observing, assessing and planning for how young children are learning. In H. Moylett (ed.), *Characteristics of Effective Early Learning*. Maidenhead: Open University Press.

Whitebread, D., Anderson, H., Coltman, P., Page, C., Pasternak, D. P. and Mehta, S. (2005) Developing independent learning in the early years. *Education 3–13*, 33, 40–50.

Whitebread, D. and Basilio, M. (2012) Emergence and early development of self-regulation in young children. *Profesorado: Journal of Curriculum and Teacher Education, Monograph issue: Learn to learn. Teaching and evaluation of self-regulated learning,* 16 (1), 15–34.

Whitebread, D., Bingham, S., Grau, V., Pasternak, D. P. and Sangster, C. (2007) Development of metacognition and self-regulated learning in young children: Role of collaborative and peer-assisted learning. *Journal of Cognitive Education and Psychology*, 6 (3), 433–455.

Whitebread, D. and O'Sullivan, L. (2012) Preschool children's social pretend play: Supporting the development of metacommunication, metacognition and self-regulation. *International Journal of Play*, 1 (2), 197–213.

Winsler, A., Diaz, R. M. and Montero, I. (1997) The role of private speech in the transition from collaborative to independent task performance in young children. *Early Childhood Research Quarterly*, 12, 59–79.

3

Valuing and celebrating small steps for children with special educational needs and disabilities

Inclusive assessment practice

Alison Lentz and Megan Panayiotou

All children are different. Many will be able to make good use of the early years provision on offer, but for others, it can be more of a challenge. We would like to introduce three young children who have attended Ronald Openshaw Nursery Education Centre (RONEC), a maintained nursery school in Stratford, East London. This will give you an idea of the importance of an accurate assessment of their very different individual needs, and how this links to celebrating each step of their learning at this critical age.

Meet Jasmine

Jasmine attends nursery for the morning sessions in a three- to four-year-old class, and has some speech delay. She was born in Thailand and spent the first six months of her life there. Jasmine is a quiet girl who found it difficult to settle into nursery. She lives at home with her mother and father, although when she first started nursery, she was being cared for by her father, paternal grandmother and aunties – her mother was not in the country due to visa issues. When her mother was able to return, she brought with her Jasmine's little sister, whom Jasmine did not know. This major change in the family dynamic unsettled Jasmine and, again, she found it difficult to separate from her mum at nursery.

Meet Malik

Malik attends the nursery school full time under Newham's pilot scheme to offer free 30-hour places for children with additional needs. He has a diagnosed autistic spectrum disorder. He receives support by being included in small group activities that focus on his speech and language needs.

Malik lives close to the nursery with his mother, grandmother and older brother and sister. He started nursery when he was two years old. Until he was three years old, Malik was non-verbal and engaged only in solitary play. He would quickly become distressed if something happened that he did not know how to deal with, such as someone taking a toy from him. He enjoys routines and will play with the same things each day, particularly enjoying the mud kitchen and dough areas. He found toilet training difficult and will still sometimes struggle with this at nursery.

Meet Annie

Annie has profound and multiple learning difficulties and has 1:1 support at all times.

Annie's early family life was disrupted by a history of parental domestic violence. Annie now resides with her mother, although her father shows some interest in her and has been allowed supervised contact. She lives with her mother in an adapted flat, with help from social services and a range of therapists who support her. A charity funds Annie to have conductive education classes,[1] which are usually only available when paid for privately.

Annie's mother cares for her well and is also addressing her own well-being by attending counselling. She is currently pregnant with Annie's baby brother, who is due in September. Annie's attendance at nursery is good and her mum has worked hard at getting her to school on time, helped by establishing a sleep routine. She helps Annie with her daily physical therapy exercises at home and ensures that she attends all appointments.

Annie started at nursery as a two-year old, having previously been in private daycare as an under two. She presented with a range of needs caused by her cerebellar hypoplasia. Her development in several prime areas had been severely delayed: she had limited mobility and her concentration and communication skills were also extremely limited. However, she was able to let us know what she enjoyed and did not enjoy by crying or smiling and laughing.

So, here we have three very different individuals with a wide range of needs.

Including children with SEND in the early years

Working in a local authority committed to the inclusion of children with special educational needs and disabilities (SEND) can be a privilege. Critical to such work, however, is a positive 'can do' approach, as opposed to one based on a deficit 'it is not possible' model.

To be inclusive, we have to acknowledge and respect the role of the parents as the child's first educators and work with them to develop a greater understanding of their child's needs. We offer support and guidance on how effective and professional relationships can be established with other services and, perhaps most importantly, recruit staff that are open to the demanding and ever-changing challenges of this work.

A 'can do' approach

Finding the most appropriate style of education is hugely important for all children, perhaps even more so for children with SEND. A mainstream education may not be the best option for the child's entire education, but if *all* children are included in well-designed early years assessments, these can provide a good starting point and be beneficial to them in the longer term. We can support parents in making decisions for their child based on a 'can do' philosophy: what *is* possible, what can be done and *how* it can be done. Such practice can change lives from a very young age.

Establishing effective partnerships with parents

A rather dated but, nonetheless, accurate comment on *developmental warning signals* is made by Mary Sheridan (1973, p. 16) when she says that the earliest indications usually depend on "mother's suspicions that her child is not seeing, hearing, moving his limbs or taking notice like other children of his age. N.B she is usually right".

Any setting begins its relationship with the child and family from the moment they register an interest, usually by putting their name on the waiting list. For assessments and placements to be successful, it is important that parents are invited to speak openly about their children – this can be difficult as parents may feel inadequate, anxious, to blame or embarrassed. If we want parents to feel comfortable enough to share what is often very emotionally upsetting information, we need to be sensitive and try to ensure that our responses do not create further obstacles. Parents of children with SEND are likely to have experienced some sort of discrimination, and this may take some time, patience and expertise to overcome.

Developing effective professional relationships

Working collaboratively with parents and outside agencies is of huge benefit – expert assessments can be made and specialised services can support staff development, which, in turn, can reduce the need for further input from such services. Most importantly, working in this positive and holistic way can help avoid children identifying with and being defined by their SEND.

An example of working well with an outside agency is the partnership that RONEC has developed with an occupational therapist (OT). She visits termly and advises the staff on ways of meeting individual needs through *sensory integration* sessions. Sensory integration is the process that helps children make sense of their body in relation to the space around them – for children with a disability, this is of crucial importance. Basic sensory experiences are those of pushing and pulling – the OT advised staff on how to develop these using a range of sensory activities, selecting relevant

equipment and learning how to position and move children safely. She did not need to advise anybody on how to have fun – that seems to come naturally! Working together in this way means staff are up-skilled and the children get daily access to the sort of opportunities they need.

Environments that do not underestimate children

Early years practitioners are very knowledgeable about young children. They know that:

- Being able to make a healthy attachment is important for a sense of security.
- Development can be sporadic and sometimes a bit up and down rather than linear.

PSED- Can talk about my abilities

I joined in with some peers who were climbing trees. I told them that I can climb trees too, as I pulled myself on to the branches.

"I can do it, I can climb watch me"

"I can go to the top like him"

"see look I did it"

- Being sociable is something that is learnt.
- Role play is how children explore their experiences and understanding of the world.
- Water play can be very calming.

The point not to be overlooked is that children with SEND are, first and foremost, children: that is, they are children with the same fundamental needs as other children. An early years environment centred on a developmental curriculum and focussing on differentiated learning is a good place for any child to start: to try it out and see what they can get out of it. Assessing how much a child is able to access such an environment is a good indicator of their initial and future trajectory in education.

Staff recruitment

Staff commitment and effectiveness is a highly significant strand of effective inclusion. Good implementation of the key worker approach contributes to the child's happiness at nursery. As with all children, the key person supporting a child with SEND needs to be sensitive and creative – the principles are exactly the same as for any child. It is worth considering Susan Isaacs's premise that "above everything else, a child needs warm human relationships, and spontaneous feelings of friendliness" (Isaacs, 1937, p. 39). When supported appropriately, accurate observations are made, children are encouraged to reflect on their work, their progress is tracked, and parents are engaged.

Supporting children with SEND may require specialist support, training and equipment. So staff need to be engaged with their own learning and development – surely, this the expectation of a practitioner anyway when responding to any of their key children, irrespective of the need at stake?

Encouraging children to self-reflect

It is important for all young children to develop skills of self-reflection, but for those with SEND, this can be more of a challenge. Encouraging children to be able to look at their work and communicate something about it may be all that is necessary to get the ball rolling. Simply having something to say, however minimal, adds a dimension of the third-person and puts in a bit of

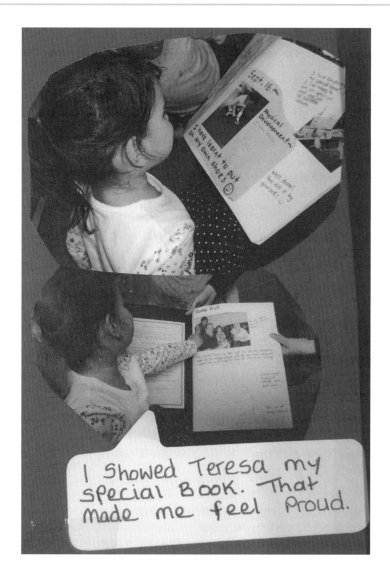

distance between them and it. Introducing this skill at a young age will stand them in good stead for the rest of their lives.

Removing barriers to learning

In Newham, the area Special Educational Needs Co-ordinators (SENCOs) are based at RONEC. The team, which is part of the Early Years SEND Hub at

RONEC, supports all of the private, voluntary and independent (PVI) settings in the borough. We have been working hard through the SEND Hub to remove barriers to children's learning and to ensure that children with SEND have equal access to early years provision. The support given, utilising the considerable expertise across Newham's Maintained Nursery School sector, includes:

- Making accurate observations of a child with SEND
- Having sensitive conversations and reviews with parents
- Recording progress and knowing when an Education and Health Care Plan (EHCP) is needed
- Making appropriate referrals to support agencies such as speech therapy
- Reflecting on the provision in place (using the Inclusive Classroom Profile[2] as a self-assessment tool)
- Applying for additional funding when necessary
- Providing training targeted at current needs, e.g. autistic spectrum disorders
- Peer coaching to share good practice between settings
- Accreditation and regular meetings for PVI SENCOs to raise the profile of this significant role
- Direct access to a speech and language therapist to give immediate advice and support

The impact of this work is seen in the notable shift in thinking from "*Can* we accommodate this child with SEND?" to "*How* can we accommodate this child with SEND?"

Including children in early years settings can help to change society – maybe only a little bit, but an important bit.

We will now go back to our three children and see what happened for them during their time at nursery.

Jasmine: initial observation (Sept 2015)

Jasmine, you have been at nursery for two weeks now but you still do not like to let go of your Gran. I see that you cling on tight until a member of staff supports you to come away. You did stop crying for a short time when you played with the bubbles in the garden, then you remembered Gran had gone and you were upset again.

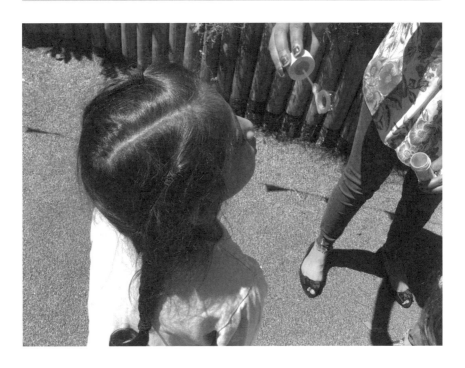

Most recent observation (Feb 2017)

Jasmine, it is lovely to see you coming into nursery ahead of your Mum and dragging her by the hand to get in quicker. You are always smiling now, such a difference from a few months ago when nursery made you so sad. I love seeing you out in the garden (your favourite place to be). I saw you today with your best friend; you were watching the rabbits in their hutch and laughing. You told your friend "look, he jump" and you both jumped around the garden pretending to be rabbits and laughing some more. You had the biggest smile on your face when I took them out of the hutch so you could stroke them and you were so gentle with them. You didn't speak to me but I could see how happy you were. Well done for finding your confidence in nursery!

By listening to Jasmine's parents, staff were able to provide targeted support for her speech and language. A huge part of her success is her growing

confidence, which has been supported by her routine experiences at nursery and her love of being outdoors.

Malik: initial observation (Sept 2015)

Malik, I could see that you enjoyed the 'communication group' today by your smiles and willingness to join in. You showed me that you do not like your tummy tickled by putting out your hand to be tickled instead. You were able to show me which song you would like us to sing by pointing to the card indicating 'the instrument song'. You joined in with all the action songs really well but I would love to hear your voice!

Most recent observation (Jan 2017)

Today, you came to play in room 6 and you amazed me with how much you have learnt since I last spent time with you. You chatted about what you had been doing, telling me, "I've been outside, it's cold!" You selected a magnetic game to play and as you sorted out the colours, you named them accurately. Suddenly, you had an idea: You said, "I'm coming back" before leaving the room. A couple of minutes later, you returned with a tape measure. You knew exactly what to do and you carefully pulled the tape across the game. I asked you how big the game board was and you confidently replied, "14". I was so impressed to see how you have been learning your numbers and how to use them in different ways. I can't wait to see what you will learn next!

Again, Malik was provided with some targeted support for speech and language – his success has been hugely supported by being able to access a wide range of nursery activities, playing with lots of other children and being able build up interactive and trusting relationships with staff.

Annie: initial observation (June 2016)

I could see you wanted to hold the Popoid figure but you were struggling to reach it. I caught hold of it for you but you showed me you did not want my help by pushing my hand away. Then you got really upset and started sobbing. You threw your glasses on the floor. You screamed and hit your hands down onto the floor.

Most recent observation (June 2017)

Annie found the water very calming and was able to regulate her emotions from waking up sad to happy and laughing. She responded to facial expressions and sounds to express her enjoyment at being splashed by the water. She was keen to lie down and dip her head underneath. Was not happy when it was time to finish but again was able to regulate her emotions with cuddles from Lara and Joan.

Annie has a lot of targeted support to meet her many and varied needs. Although she has always been able to express her feelings, she is now harnessing this to indicate preference: this could sound like a small step, but it is one of huge significance for Annie.

Celebrating Children's Learning through assessment

The purpose of the assessment process is to make explicit children's achievements, celebrate these with them and help them to move forward on to their next goal. Observing the children is an important tool for all staff. It is important, too, to share this with the child – when this is done, assessment information is more likely to result in a raising of standards, because the child is more focused, motivated and aware of her or his own capabilities. Good assessment practice enables children to be able to fulfil their learning potential and raises self-esteem and self-confidence.

(Hutchin, 1996, p. 9)

Assessing the progress of children with SEND in the early years requires creativity and flexibility: every setting will have an assessment system based on the Early Years Foundation Stage framework, and there will be some standard activities that lend themselves well to observing what individuals have learnt. As Diane Rochford has argued:

An inclusive system accommodating as many pupils as possible allows for progression within it and provides continuity across different educational settings. It also facilitates the development of shared good practice. Wherever possible, pupils should have access to mainstream statutory assessment arrangements.

(Department for Education, 2016, p. 6)

Whilst Rochford (2016) is referring to pupils aged over five, the principle is still the same for our younger children. In fact, one of the review's key recommendations could be read as a description of the very nature and ethos of the Early Years Foundation Stage. Diane Rochford recommends a new statutory duty:

[T]o assess pupils not engaged in curriculum-specific learning against the following 7 aspects of cognition and learning and report this to parents and carers: responsiveness, curiosity, discovery, anticipation, persistence, initiation and investigation.

(Department for Education, 2016, p. 6)

It seems, then, that we early years practitioners are very well placed to gather the relevant information from which to draw an informed, accurate and relevant assessment of a child with a complex special educational need or disability.

What does 'progress' look like on paper for children with complex needs?

Annie

The real difference in Annie's development began to show when she took a full-time place. Her physical skills began to develop rapidly and she went from learning to hold up her head whilst in a tummy position to pulling herself to a standing position within a few months. This progress was easy to see: we all celebrated her achievements as she started to crawl towards her toys and friends.

Her personal, social and emotional development could also be seen as she began to smile, reach out to her peers and develop a strong bond with her key person. She began to gain a real sense of independence with a 'can do' attitude and now insists on doing what she wants to do when she wants to do it.

The area in which it was harder to see her progress was that of communication. According to our standard nursery system for analysing assessment information, one year after being at nursery, she had made no progress. All those who worked with Annie knew that progress had been made and it was important to be able to evidence this. So we decided to use the specialist BSquared assessment software package (designed for children with special needs), which was able to show the tiny, but hugely significant, steps of her progress. By having four stages of development for each statement, even the smallest amount of progress can be measured. For example, the birth–11 months stage for Communication and Language: Speaking in *Development Matters* is described as:

- Communicates needs and feelings in a variety of ways including crying, gurgling, babbling and squealing

- Makes own sounds in response when talked to by familiar adults
- Lifts arms in anticipation of being picked up
- Practises and gradually develops speech sounds (babbling) to communicate with adults; says sounds like 'baba, nono, gogo'

(Early Education, 2012, p. 19)

Annie might be in early years provision for quite some time before this band would represent the 'best fit' for her development. So showing progress might take years. However, BSquared breaks this stage down into much smaller steps of progress, including:

- Makes soft gurgling sounds
- Responds to human voice with gentle guttural sounds
- Gurgles when contented
- Attempts to initiate intentional communication
- Cries for attention
- Demonstrates an awareness that crying brings a response
- Indicates different needs with different noises
- Vocalises to gain attention
- Screams when annoyed
- Vocalises to an adult
- Vocalises two different sounds

In one year, Annie went from having achieved 21% of the 0–11 month age band to mastering over 80% a year later (according to the BSquared system). This demonstrates the critical importance of choosing the assessment process carefully for each individual child in order to notice and celebrate the progress they have made.

The following observations show in richer detail what we mean by saying that Annie's use of gestures to communicate has moved from the stage of 'engaged" to 'involved':

Whilst looking at the book Brown Bear, Brown Bear *with her friend, Annie tried to turn the page before her friend was ready. Her friend pushed Annie's hand away. Annie has encountered the pushing-away gesture to indicate* **no**.

Several days later, Annie's key person noted that:

> *I could see you wanted to hold the Popoid figure but you were strug-*
> *gling to reach it. I caught hold of it for you but you showed me you did*
> *not want my help by pushing my hand away.*

This shows that Annie can now use a gesture (pushing her key person's hand away) to communicate her meaning ('I don't want your help'). Now that Annie is using a gesture to communicate, she is assessed as having moved from 'engaged' to 'involved'.

Celebrating children's learning with parents

At RONEC, our data is important to us – it informs us of those areas in which our children are making progress and those on which we need to focus. It also enables us to compare our provision with settings around us – we can then support each other and draw on the strengths of our peers. As a staff team, we considered carefully how important it was to share this raw data with parents. We decided not to do so, although it is available to them on request, as we prefer to share the child's progress in a way that does not involve a 'label' regarding the developmental age/stage band they happen to lie in. We do this in a variety of ways:

- First and foremost, we celebrate each incremental step as it happens. Peers are encouraged to support each other and cheer each other on when try-ing something new. All progress is shared verbally with parents at the end of the day or written in their home/school communication book.
- The 'bigger' achievements are celebrated in our sharing group time with the whole nursery.
- Another way we record progress is through the child's individual Special Book: a visual record of activities that the child has participated in, work they have created and steps they have taken. These books are designed to be easily accessible to both parents and children. Annie's books, for instance, are bright and colourful and the photographs are printed out in a large size to enable her to see them more clearly. Annie, too, has a

memory stick where movies of her achievements are stored. These are seen by Annie, her mother and the other key professionals at her review meetings – an explicit way of enabling everyone to see her progress.

- On a more formal level, at the end of each term, the key person will write a summary drawing together all key achievements. This is shared during parents' week and parents are invited to add their comments.
- Detailed support plans are in place that clearly state what is going well, what needs further work and any progress towards longer-term goals.

At the end of the year, key professionals such as the nursery school staff, physiotherapists, occupational therapists, speech and language therapists, and social services meet with the parents to discuss the progress made over the year. The key documents looked at are the Special Books, video films and any further feedback from professionals and the family.

Having said all that, an ongoing question and area of reflection for us is always 'have we got the balance right?' Below is an excerpt from a parent's feedback about how we demonstrate the progress of children with complex special educational needs and disabilities at RONEC:

> I'm extremely lucky and happy that my son has had the opportunity to attend this nursery with wonderful teachers who are doing an amazing job. He has had very good close relationships with his keyworker because we were sharing all information and monitoring every step he took together. Sharing and doing this together helped him to make huge progress: we celebrated every little step. As a parent I feel that the most useful information regarding his progress was one to one conversations, movies and particularly his special book. You can easily follow, step by step, his improvement. The times I met with the SENCO were enough due to the feedback I received every day. Thank you all for your hard work.
>
> Lina Pranskunaite, 2016

Notes

1 Conductive education is based on the work of Hungarian Professor András Pető. It has been specifically developed for children and adults who have motor disorders of neurological origin such as cerebral palsy.

2 The Inclusive Classroom Profile (ICP) is a structured observation rating scale designed to assess the quality of provisions and daily classroom practices that support the developmental needs of children with disabilities in early childhood settings.

References

Department for Education (2016) *The Rochford Review: Final Report* (Online). www.gov.uk/government/uploads/system/uploads/attachment_data/file/561411/Rochford_Review_Report_v5_PFDA.pdf (Last accessed 27 July 2017)

Early Education (2012) *Development Matters in the Early Years Foundation Stage* (Online). www.early-education.org.uk/development-matters (Last accessed 27 July 2017)

Hutchin, V. (1996) *Tracking Significant Achievement in the Early Years*. London: Hodder and Stoughton.

Isaacs, S. (1937) *The Educational Value of the Nursery School*. London: The Nursery School Association of Great Britain.

Sheridan, M. (1973) *Children's Developmental Progress From Birth to Five Years*. Windsor: NFER.

4

Assessment in diverse contexts
Talking with Bangladeshi-British parents about children's early learning
Tania Choudhury

Lipa grew up in a small neighbourhood in Comila, Bangladesh. She lived in Italy for some time with her husband and son before giving birth to her daughter in her early 40s. This was a complicated birth, and her daughter underwent major reconstructive surgery. The family then migrated to the UK sometime later in hope of a better life and greater opportunities. As she spoke fondly of her child's experiences in playing outdoors, she recalled her own earliest memory of play. Running under the mango trees and seeking shelter from the heavy monsoon, she had once believed that this was a separate world from school, this was fun and play, not learning. But years later, she grew to believe that there is in fact great value in play, particularly for her youngest child, who had experienced traumatic early years and was a selective mute. She accredits this change in her thinking to the engagement with the nursery school her daughter attends:

> Learning through play is the best way to learn. You tap into their interests. This worked for my daughter. I saw the way in which her key person tuned into her interests, listened to what I had to say and then won her trust. This was important for my daughter and now she is confident. She talks about what she does at school with so much joy. I learnt a lot from speaking to the teacher and seeing for myself what you do and how you understand my child.

Introduction

The early years is often the envy of other phases of education due to the level of parental involvement compared with later years. Experienced and new teachers alike discuss the difficulty of speaking to parents when their children are in the upper phases. This is often due to practical reasons such as timing and staffing, but parents seem to be more willing to be present when their child is younger. It could be argued, however, that this envy is a result of recognising just how significant an impact there can be when the two arenas of the home and the school interact in order to appreciate and develop the child as a learner.

In the light of the recent Assessment without Levels report (Department for Education, 2015), which calls for the dissolution of thresholds and for schools to create their own assessment models, it appears that there is an onus on schools to work with parents to support formative assessment from the early years onwards. If the idea that "there is no intrinsic value in recording formative assessment; what matters is that it is acted on" (Department for Education, 2015, p. 30) is to be truly meaningful, then formative assessment must go beyond the school and involve parents. Many examples are demonstrated in this chapter.

However, parents are not a simple homogenous group of people, especially in diverse areas like East London where I work as a teacher. Are black and minority ethnic (BME) parents properly involved in sharing and discussing formative assessment information about their children? I would argue that there seems to be a worrying gap in the engagement of this group of parents. A space for dialogue has not been created, and this is preventing formative approaches to assessment from being developed.

In this chapter, I will start by exploring some of the reasons why this gap between the engagement with those easier-to-reach families and BME families exists. I will then move on to capturing how a group of Bangladeshi-British parents talk about their children's early learning. Throughout, I take into consideration the different cultural backgrounds and expectations of this particular group, and demonstrate how their voices impacted my practice and consequently the children's development. I will be describing some of my journey to develop dialogue about formative assessment with an often marginalised community.

Literature review

At government policy level, the importance of working with parents has been discussed at length from as early as the 1967 Plowden report. This stated that "one of the essentials for educational advance is a close partnership between the two parties [school and home] to every child's education . . . There is certainly an association between parental encouragement and educational performance" (Central Advisory Council for Education, 1967). In more recent times, the Early Excellence and Sure Start Children's Centre programmes, developed from 1997 onwards, emphasised the crucial role of parental involvement in the early years. Over the years, more reports have emerged such as Better Schools for All (Department for Education, 2005) and then Every Parent Matters (Department for Education, 2007b) and The Children's Plan (Department for Education, 2007a) in the same year, with government policy continuing to emphasise the crucial importance of parental engagement.

On an academic level, the monumental Effective Provision of Pre-school Education (EPPE) project (Sylva et al., 2004), led by a group of key researchers in early years education, demonstrated the significance of the home learning environment and parental engagement. The EPPE project found that effective pre-school education included a strong partnership with parents. It was the quality of home learning that mattered, regardless of family background or wealth: "for all children, the quality of the home learning environment is more important for intellectual and social development than parental occupation, education or income. What parents do is more important than who parents are" (Sylva et al., 2004, p. ii).

The sister project, Researching Effective Pedagogy in the Early Years (REPEY, Siraj-Blatchford et al., 2002), also drew links between the rapid progress of a child and their home learning environment. The researchers found from interviews with 100 parents that when parents and staff held a shared educational aim and children were being supported at home, then effective learning occurred, particularly for middle-class settings. In the context of the nursery school that I am based at, most children are eligible for free school meals and most belong to BME families and so in light of the findings of this project, it can be assumed that many of these children may not do as well as those of middle-class families. So whilst the EPPE project found that "what parents do is more important than who parents are" (Sylva et al., 2004, p. ii), we need to ask if there has there been adequate engagement with BME parents to support the development of pedagogic efforts at home.

Garry Hornby (2011) notes different models in which schools engage parents, including the consumer model, transmission model and curriculum-enrichment model. The most recommended model, however, and certainly the most apt for the early years environment, is the school-parent partnership approach. This consists of teachers and early years educators who are experts on early learning working in collaboration with parents who are experts on their children. As a result, the best outcomes for the child will be achieved.

Chris Athey, who headed the Froebel Early Education Project in the 1970s, is best-known for the development of 'schema theory' (Athey, 1990). She suggests that patterns of behaviour – or schemas – are encouraged by innate cognitive structures. For example, if a child likes spinning around in the garden, and will spend periods of time observing the washing machine and continue to draw circles, then they could be interpreted as having a circulatory schema. The identification of the schema, argues Athey, can lead to well-informed next steps. But this project also has much to tell us about parental involvement.

Athey arranged three-hour morning sessions with parents every week for two years where they would visit a range of places, or be visited – a significant investment in the parent-teacher partnership. As Athey famously concluded: "Parents and professionals can help children separately or work together to the great benefit of the children. Parents can give practical help in the classrooms (as many already do), but perhaps the greatest benefit to teachers in working with parents is to aspire towards making their own pedagogy conscious and explicit" (Athey, 2007, p. 209).

Likewise, Bronfenbrenner and Condry's ecological system (1978) depicts the child at the core whilst all other systems function around them; I would argue that this model of the unique child at the centre with the school and parents uniting to ensure optimum success should be at the heart of our practice when working with children and families (see Figure 4.1).

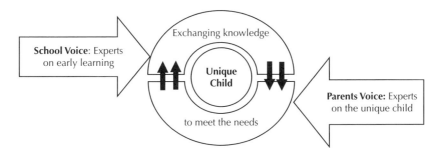

Figure 4.1

Adapted from Bronfenbrenner and Condry (1978)

However, the voices and experiences of those parents defined as 'hard to reach', in relation to assessing children's learning, have not been adequately investigated in recent times, with BME families being particularly neglected. One seminal exception is Liz Brooker's (2002) comparative study into the early experiences of Bangladeshi, Anglo and dual heritage families when their child started school. Brooker found that a level of institutional racism that existed towards Bangladeshi families caused the school to focus blame about the children's poor progress on to the parents. The children were consequently marginalised from the majority, despite the policies and school ethos that allegedly welcomed them. It is scary to think that such practices continued as late as after the millennium, and within a diverse community. Perhaps more worrying, too, is that there seemed little desire to overcome these barriers and develop a relationship between home and school.

Similarly, the findings from Ogilvy et al.'s (1990) research into a Scottish nursery school illustrate the dangers of making assumptions about BME children and families. In this study, it was found that the nursery staff interacted differently with Scottish children compared to Asian children. One member of staff is quoted as saying, 'It'll be like getting blood out of a stone' – demonstrating a crude assumption about engaging with Asian children. Asian children were spoken about as a group rather than seen as individuals, unlike the Scottish children. Such attitudes within a setting would now be regarded as highly discriminatory and controversial; this begs the question of whether people are now better at masking their opinions or whether there has been a genuine development in how practitioners think about children of different ethnicities. Nonetheless, that practitioners interacted in a negative way with children from a minority group is a truly shocking finding. If such attitudes are still rife, then that goes against the British values of equality and respect that we teach our children, and are so hot on the agenda.

In Daniele Joly's 1984 study into the opinions of Mirpuri parents in Saltley, Birmingham, about their children's schooling, she found that most parents expressed the desire for their child to access a good education so that they could receive relevant certificates to gain jobs in high positions. However, the absence of a shared language led to difficulty in accessing information about how their child was performing, a barrier they felt could be overcome by the employment of Asian teachers at the school.

The language barrier was also recognised by Paula Hamilton (2013) in her study of how Eastern European families were integrated into two schools in North Wales. The language barrier was found to be the greatest obstacle in preventing parental engagement. In terms of parental aspirations, Hamilton found that parents were also interested in providing their children with a more didactic learning experience than was offered by the Welsh schools, and experienced anxieties that their children would lag behind and have to be taught with younger children if they moved to other countries.

A chapter on parental involvement is incomplete without the mention of Margy Whalley's work at the Pen Green Centre – a nursery, teaching school, research base and community hub. As the director of the research centre and the Pen Green programme called 'Parents' Involvement in their Children's Learning (PICL)', Whalley demonstrated the positive outcomes of working closely with families using a community education model (Whalley, 2017). In this comprehensive study, Whalley worked with many at the centre to develop practice about how to actively engage parents and understand the reasons why some may find this more difficult than others. The project is a testimony to why Whalley and the Pen Green Centre in Corby are so exemplary. It also sheds light on some of their attempts to understand families and the value of this in terms of developing a shared understanding of each child as a learner.

In conclusion, there is a growing evidence base showing how important it is for schools and settings to engage with parents, and the significant benefits as a result of these relationships. There is also evidence to suggest that parents of BME families, often regarded to be 'hard to reach', do host aspirations for their children to do well at school. What I aimed to do was to marry these spheres together.

Engaging with Bangladeshi-British parents

Bearing in mind how valuable the parent-school partnership is, I engaged with the parents from the Bangladeshi-British community at Sheringham Nursery School in East London, where I teach, in order to gain an understanding of the way they speak about their children's learning and identify their challenges. But I further extended this, responding to what parents said by making changes to my pedagogy and aiming to develop higher-quality practice.

The Bangladeshi-British community in the UK

Ofsted's report into the Achievement of Bangladeshi Heritage Pupils (2004) found that some parents could not understand school reports, and that this was a significant obstacle in discussions between the school and home about the child's progress and performance. Some parents are described as enjoying seeing what their children had learnt, but feeling unable to support or contribute to their child's learning. When the report makes statements like "the parents wanted the best for their children and felt that it was the school's job to ensure that this objective was fulfilled, rather than theirs" (Ofsted, 2004, p. 11), it could be argued that this is a highly simplistic viewpoint, presenting the British Bangladeshi community as a homogenous group.

I have chosen to focus on the British Bangladeshi community in this chapter for a range of reasons, mainly driven by the context of the nursery school in which I am based and my own Bengali heritage. Practical considerations, such as my ability to translate and work within pre-established relationships, enable me to hear and provide a richer and more authentic voice. I am also mindful that the size of the Bangladeshi community is growing in our setting, which makes it all the more relevant to hear some of the unheard voices.

The Bangladeshi community's first major wave of migration to England was in the 1960s, when men – the majority from the quiet rural region of Sylhet – migrated in the hope of a better life. Their wives and children followed in turn, leading to the growth of the community. Within the last decade, a new influx has emerged, with Bangladeshis who originate from the more urban regions of Bangladesh like Dhaka, the country's capital, entering the UK via other European countries such as Italy. This provides an interesting context for my study: there are now distinct diversities within the community itself with first, second and third generations living amongst each other, with a greater variety of experiences compared to those from the first wave of migration.

Case studies of parents

For the research for this chapter, I invited a varied range of Bangladeshi parents at Sheringham Nursery School to take part in an interview on the subject of their children's early learning. The majority were willing but due to time constraints, some were unable to commit. I conducted semi-structured interviews with the six parents who participated, some of which were conducted in their home language and then translated. I tried to gather a group that was varied but representative. Table 4.1 contains some key information relating to the parents:

Table 4.1 Case study participants

Name	Gender	Age	Length in UK	Lives with	Originally from	Education level	Current employment	Past employment	Interview translated
Askir	M	36	Since birth	Wife and daughter	Sylhet, Bangladesh	Diploma, BA, MA, Mphil, PhD	Teacher/Lecturer	N/A	No
Dilwara	F	30	11 years	Husband and two sons	India	Higher Secondary Education (India) ESOL Entry 3	Unemployed	Marketing	No
Lipa	F	46	3 years	Husband, son and daughter	Comilla, Bangladesh	BA (Bangladesh) Childcare Level 1 ESOL Entry Level 2	Unemployed	Teaching Assistant	Yes
Sultana	F	33	Since birth	Husband, two daughters and extended family	Sylhet, Bangladesh	GCSE, A Levels	Unemployed	Housing officer	No
Tara	F	34	9 years	Husband and daughter	Dhaka, Bangladesh	BA in Fashion Design (Bangladesh) BA in Business Administration	Unemployed	Costume assistant and fashion designer	No
Zuleyka	F	28	6 years	Husband, two daughters and a son	Sylhet, Bangladesh	Higher Secondary Education (Bangladesh)	Unemployed	N/A	Yes

Askir

Askir is a British-born Bangladeshi who is a teacher at an international school in Central London. He occasionally lectures at universities, has a PhD, organises international museum exhibitions and studied Arabic abroad. Askir meets with us when relevant to talk about his daughter's progress, but as he works full time, these meetings occur infrequently and his wife manages the day-to-day picking up and more informal briefings. His daughter has a diagnosis of autism spectrum disorder (ASD) and both parents are well aware of their daughter's needs and how to meet them.

Dilwara

Dilwara's family migrated from Sylhet to a small town in India before settling in the UK. She identifies herself as being both Bengali and Indian and speaks the Sylheti dialect. Dilwara grew up in the city and is a Hindu by faith, unlike the large majority of Bangladeshi migrants who are Muslim. Despite this, she has good relations with other Bangladeshi parents at the setting. She is currently unemployed due to childcare and is expecting her third child.

Lipa

Lipa grew up in the urban city of Comilla in Bangladesh, where she obtained a university degree. After arriving in the UK via Italy, she studied childcare and English as an Additional Language, before working as a teaching assistant. She is currently unemployed, which she explains is due to childcare. However, she regularly volunteers at the school's weekly Forest School in order to keep her expertise current. She lives at home with her husband and two children and hopes to return to work once her child settles into school full time.

Sultana

Sultana is a British-born Bangladeshi and one of eight children. She grew up in Brick Lane, Tower Hamlets, an area heavily populated by the first wave of Bangladeshis. She now lives in Newham. Previously, Sultana had worked as a housing officer at a local council, working part time after returning from maternity leave after her first child and then eventually leaving this job to manage childcare commitments. She lives with her husband, two daughters and extended family in a large house near the school, and is currently expecting her third child.

Tara

Tara was born in Dhaka, Bangladesh, where she attended a missionary school, an English school, and then a Bengali school before completing a degree in Fashion Design. Tara states that she had originally studied English Literature due to family pressure, but changed her mind after her first year and opted to pursue her true passion instead. She married her long-distance partner of 10 years who was based in the UK, and moved to London where she has been living for the past nine years. Tara is currently in the process of establishing her own business and attends many evening courses at the London College of Fashion to keep up to date with the latest trends.

Zuleyka

Zuleyka was born in a village in Sylhet, Bangladesh, and arrived in the UK as a result of an arranged marriage, a similar story to many of the first wave of migrants in the '60s. She was educated to secondary level in Bangladesh and has never worked. She lives with her husband, three children and extended family. Zuleyka does not have any of her own family in the UK.

Emerging trends – discussions

The child – past and present

Historically, the child in the Bangladeshi community was viewed in a very different light to the contemporary child in Britain. Many of the parents who took part in this research project experienced this. Dilwara, Lipa and Zuleyka particularly highlighted the fact that their parents were strict and did not allow them to make their own choices: *"It is completely different now. We didn't get anything . . . it was so difficult,"* said Zuleyka. *"My parents were very strict. They wouldn't even let us go to the shops . . . everything bought would be of their choice,"* Dilwara added. Regarding expectations as a result of such an upbringing, Askir said: *"I studied Philosophy and they were like 'what, what was that – doctor of medicine?',"* implying that such jobs are held in high regard in the community. The parents also spoke about how expectations were imposed especially on males to get qualifications for high-status jobs. This claim was supported by the findings of Joly (1984) and Ofsted's report into Bangladeshi heritage pupils (Ofsted, 2004), where interviews revealed the high ambitions parents held for their children. This may suggest that within the community, Bangladeshi children are – or perhaps *were* – seen by their parents as being vehicles for furthering social status, hence the great emphasis on submission to ensure they follow the guidance of their parents' ambitions for them. The emerging trends that I discovered during my discussions with parents therefore proved to be unlike those I had anticipated. Instead of recycling historic views, their views appear to show a shift away from the traditional submissive model of the child.

Celebrating confidence and independence: a new trend?

The relevance of understanding how children are traditionally viewed in Bengali culture emerges in this section. It appears from discussing with parents that there is a new trend in how parents talk about and assess their children's learning. Personal, social and emotional development is arguably the most significant aspect of development in the early years. Having spoken to all of the parents, a key theme that stood out was how they celebrated their children's achievements in this area the most. In contrast, they showed differing attitudes on learning through play. For all the parents, this celebration of confidence and independence took precedence over learning numbers and letters, potentially a step away from the strict didactic model of parenting that had previously been glorified in their communities.

Parents spoke about their children's growing confidence as the greatest accomplishment at nursery and how they acknowledge that this skill equips them for later life. "*When the confidence grows, then the children can do more things and learn more. That is the main achievement,*" said Lipa as two other parents nodded and murmured in agreement. She then added, "*Sometimes, if they want something of their choice and are confident of it, then that too is admirable, that they are defiant, feisty and can freely share an opinion.*" The subject of listening to the child's voice will be explored in greater depth in the next section, yet what Lipa has stated indicates that parents have responded to the emphasis placed in the nursery on children being able to voice their opinions with confidence.

Tara cites an instance when her child had developed confidence over time and how she regards this as the ultimate learning priority for her child:

My daughter used to get scared of all the flies like, 'I can't touch that mud – I can't go to that swing'. She gets very scared . . . she used to be actually but now she's changing because she's picking up all the things here [nursery] from the kids. That's the particular thing I want for my daughter. To be brave. Not the education wise to be the topper.

Tara suggests therefore that she does not measure her child's achievement by a grade or a developmental band, but rather qualitatively through the progress she sees long term in her emotional development. Her daughter's achievement is celebrated as being individual and personalised.

Likewise, Askir could relate to this confidence in his own daughter and demonstrates how this has manifested itself into her day-to-day experiences:

I can say she has this independent streak. She does things for herself. Maybe I don't see it every day incrementally . . . I see it when it's come to its end, its fruition and I might say it's the obvious but getting up, dressing herself, going to the bathroom, brushing her teeth . . . even though it's all over her nose at the end of it but she wouldn't let me or mum do it for her. She's like, 'No no, I'm gonna do it' – whatever it is she will do it herself. Even if it might take longer than other children . . . but she does it herself. So I found that quite remarkable. Even if it might be unorthodox. That shocked me – she can actually do that.

For Askir, this seems to be especially significant, perhaps due to his daughter having a diagnosis of ASD. He recognises that differentiation is necessary for her progression. He shows how he is an expert on his child as he later elaborates on this, talking about how his understanding of her progress is different to what his parents would have been:

I'm not personally interested in her achievement on paper. I'm more sort of interested in seeing her qualitatively develop. I'm not a competitive parent, I'm really not. My parents relatively were I suppose and it's understandable. I don't see anything wrong with that because competition can be very good in some instances. But with regards to my daughter, I'm wanting to see qualitative development over time. Not that the teacher saying she's the best in the class, or the teacher saying that she's drawn the best picture or I don't know . . . that she made the best building block. But more qualitative development. Is she gaining, substantiating her understanding, learning and cognitive processes – so that is important.

Askir therefore presents an understanding that assessment is not limited to bands and is more about observations made over time between the school and parents, sharing knowledge in order to inform one another. When I asked what motivated this idea, he referred to the International Baccalaureate assessment that was now being used in his school: his work as a teacher had impacted his viewpoint as a parent.

Tara provided an example where her daughter showed independence that really surprised her, but unlike Askir, she does make reference to an age band:

Sometimes, she is cooking. She will say, 'Ok mum, give me the footstool' and I'm thinking, oh my god she will burn her hand but yeah she did it, but I gave her the knife . . . not sharp but she chopped it and made the soup. So surprised. Look at her age, she is four years old and doing these things. My family, my whole family whenever they see her, they get surprised.

It appears, from this example, that because the nursery incorporates knives into the home corner and engages children in cooking activities, these skills have now penetrated the home learning environment. Tara captures the anxiety that many parents face when allowing their child to take risks. As a means of acknowledging Tara's anxieties, I invited her to join her daughter for an outdoor cooking session on the fire pit at nursery, where she could witness how comfortable adults can be when engaging children in activities that involve an element of risk. Later, she expressed that she is now a lot more confident when cooking with her daughter. Her daughter is now directing the cooking and talking about the processes involved, healthy eating and handling tools safely. This sharing of knowledge helped, then, to develop the child's interests and thus support and extend her learning. Potentially, this conversation with the parent could have occurred in a 10-minute, once-a-term discussion of the child's summative assessment, with the teacher informing Tara that her child is at the 30–50 month age band and in order to develop to 40–60, she may need to do this or that. It would seem clear, however, that the prior scenario is undoubtedly more effective: actually involving the parent and having immediate and intimate discussions on a regular basis as opposed to cramming all that is to be said in a rare meeting. This is an example of high-quality formative assessment, with parent and teacher working together and encouraging a continuity of learning at home by overcoming cultural challenges.

Risk taking and developing confidence and independence is a core value of Sheringham Nursery School, and this has been shared with the parents in various ways. Forest School is a prime example. Parents have been invited to volunteer with the weekly Forest School where children learn to use various tools to create things, climb trees and engage in bug hunts. The sessions are valuable for the children, who have often not experienced such close proximity with nature due to their housing or their parents' own perspectives regarding its purpose and significance. But they are also insightful for the parent volunteers, who get to witness other adults who are comfortable with children taking risks and get to see just how capable children are at being independent.

Lipa shares her view on how she has noticed the impact of Forest School on children's confidence:

> Whenever I have taken my children to the park, I have said, 'Get on that swing', but I learnt that actually with friends they are climbing trees, and I have seen that at Forest School. I have seen that confidence in the children myself, which I didn't see before. That attitude you [the nursery] refer to as. . . 'I can do things myself' and they share this at home with their siblings and parents that they have learnt this and they can do this.

Lipa refers to one of the Characteristics of Effective Learning in the Early Years Foundation Stage (EYFS), having a 'can-do' attitude. Her ability to apply this in context demonstrates the effectiveness of a dialogue about her child's learning. Lipa is now more attuned to her daughter's skills as a learner – this forms a good basis for further engaging her in supporting her daughter's learning at home.

The discussions appear to suggest that Bengali parents at Sheringham Nursery School are in tune with their children's personal, social and emotional development and regard risk taking and independence to be some of the most valuable learning points in the early years. Moreover, as the instance with Tara suggests, it is through exchanging knowledge that a formative assessment – that is assessment for learning – can truly occur.

Listen to our voices – 'those who listen do well'

On entry to Sheringham Nursery School, children are assessed in only four areas, two of which are about communication and language. Parents contribute to this assessment, which is based on what the child is doing at home as well as in nursery. This approach to dialogue around assessment and progress continues throughout the year. Communication and language is highly emphasised at the nursery school and staff are trained in the Every Child a Talker (ECAT) programme. Although to begin with, summative assessment with age bands is used, the follow-up assessment for learning takes place through what practitioners observe and act upon. When a child is noticed to be doing something, the adult – rather than standing silently and recording this – may intervene and extend the learning through facilitating sustained shared thinking (Siraj-Blatchford et al., 2002), or providing additional resources or language. The Vygotskyian notion of the 'zone of proximal development' (1978) and Jerome Bruner's (Wood, Bruner and Ross, 1976) concept of scaffolding come into mind: it is important for adults to know when it is necessary to intervene and extend. Our nursery planning is based on the children's interests with increasingly more planning for 'in the moment' interventions. This encourages immediate extension of the child's initial activity and thought processes to occur and, as such, promotes the Characteristics of Effective Learning (Early Education, 2012). Taking this into account along with the knowledge shared with the parent, this is formative assessment in action. However, from the discussions with the parents, it appeared that whilst as staff we understand and value this theory greatly, it was not the same for parents.

When discussing the most significant characteristic of a good learner, the sample group agreed that it was 'good listening'. In the parents own voices: *"Package of things but one thing that makes a learner a good learner . . . listening skills,"* stated Askir. His view was common with other parents. *"Listening and eye contact [as qualities of a good learner] rather than talking too much, which she does. But she does listen a lot,"* said Tara. *"I think listening is important too,"* agreed Dilwara, *"If they listen, then they will learn. In my opinion, listening is the most important quality of a good learner."* Zuleyka adds: *"I too like them think the same. Their mind is very important. And if their mind tells them to listen to parents, then this is important."* Sultana also contributes by adding, *"Good concentration, a little bit of discipline, know when to listen to do certain things, I guess."* And Lipa firmly concluded with, *"Those who listen do well."*

Rather than think of working in conjunction with the child and developing their skills through a conversation and sustained shared thinking, it seems that the parents think the practice of the child listening to an adult is the most important. However, it is relevant to remember that many of these parents endured a traditional, submissive form of childhood themselves.

It is interesting to note that the Characteristics of Effective Learning in the EYFS do not highlight listening. That is not to downplay the value of listening, as it is a prime skill to attain, but there are other significant ways to help the individual learner. For example, there was a child at Sheringham Nursery School who found sitting and listening very challenging and this would often lead to violent behaviour. He found the environment difficult and did not like to be led by an adult. He had a great passion for the Mobilo construction set and would spend long periods of time engaged in play, really concentrating, paying attention to details and problem solving. As a practitioner, I acted on that information to tap into his interests and to help him to develop as a learner. Through his mastery of Mobilo play, I ensured that he also developed social skills such as turn-taking, interacting with peers and eventually negotiating. This interest was shared with his mother, who then purchased Mobilo construction toys so that she could recreate this experience at home, to continue the support around the development of his social skills and language. However, through speaking to the parents of the sample group, the idea of shared sustained thinking does not appear to have taken hold: they still hold the idea that listening is the most significant way to learn.

Whilst listening is certainly an integral quality in communication and language, this should not stifle the child's voice and this has been emphasised at Sheringham Nursery School through the use of Special Books. The Special Books at nursery are large portfolios that capture the children's learning through pictures and observations. One of the aims of the books is to encourage parental understanding of key elements in the EYFS and showcase what and how their child is learning. Ultimately, the Special Book is seen as belonging to the child and so it prominently features their voice. Through weekly conferencing, children revisit and recall their experiences with their key person, developing metacognition and language that is then noted in the book. The child's voice is therefore very apparent. From a parental perspective, Dilwara stated, "*I have written what [my son] has done and said like when he went to the park,*" indicating that the child's voice in context of the Special Books is valued and understood in this household. Likewise, Sultana said: "*I have borrowed it twice so far. We stick pictures together, talk about the pictures, we go through teacher's comments and write extra notes of what she says. Yeah, she is so proud of it. Obviously, I'm not there to see what she is doing and there are pictures of her playing with children as well. It is good to see that."* The other parents in the sample group, however, did not contribute to the Special Book by capturing their child's voice, but instead recorded just their own comments – which are, of course, also greatly valued.

Askir spoke highly of the development in learning that can be seen in the Special Books: *"It gave me a chance to look back and say, oh my god, she was doing this and now look what she's doing. Even though it might not be the whole story, it's still a story."* "I really like the Special Book. What they do, what they say, what has been taught – all this is present. I really like the Special Book a lot. I have always thought that I would wrap it up and present it as a gift on his birthday when he is older,"* commented Dilwara enthusiastically. Zuleyka agreed with her, *"The Special Books are special for us too,"* she added, *"We get to know what our children are learning."* It appears that parents recognise the relevance of the book in conveying the learning that is taking place at nursery.

This was highlighted further when Dilwara dwelled upon how the Special Book would have impacted her childhood had it existed in her time: *"It would have been good because they could know we are learning something at school and helped us. But they [parents] didn't get anything at school and so didn't teach us anything either."* I find it groundbreaking that she recognises how the Special Book serves as a bridge between the two parties: Dilwara appears to make a link between what is learnt at school and 'help' offered at home.

In the Special Book of Askir's daughter, there is an entry made by Askir and his wife that indicates her current interest in puzzles. I used this knowledge shared by the parents to direct her to more challenging wooden puzzles in order to develop her thinking skills. She eventually mastered the puzzles by asking for support from her friends – a massive accomplishment considering that when she first started nursery, she only engaged in solitary play. Furthermore, due to her diagnosis of ASD, she has an Early Years Support plan: one of her targets around communication and language is to engage in conversation with peers. Because her parents informed the nursery of what her current interests were at home and what she liked speaking about, this could then be extended at nursery. The Special Book enables this invaluable exchanging of information, and noting of the child's development over time.

Nevertheless, Lipa had reservations about how the parent's voice was recorded in the Special Book:

> One day, I was given the Special Book with a yellow bubble, told that as you like, you can insert a comment here. I felt like I had to write a comment there, so I did . . . I think an empty space is better. If there is a picture that especially interests me and I just want to write some-thing there, then that is better.

Lipa suggests that she felt her voice was being directed, whereas she would prefer to comment freely on any aspect of her child's learning rather than what the practitioner was guiding her towards. She wanted autonomy over her contribution. Lipa's feedback was shared with my team and now staff are encouraged to give parents more open-ended freedom to comment yet still offer suggestions to those parents who they feel may benefit from them.

Through follow-up discussions, a greater emphasis has been placed on parents recognising and noting their children's voices at home. As a result, dialogue between the parent and child based on the child's learning experience is now captured in the books by some parents. This is something that did not occur before and is hopefully a move towards sustained shared thinking. Parents' attention has also been drawn to the teacher-child conversations that are scribed in the Special Books during conferencing – these can be used as models for the forms of conversations between parents and their children.

To challenge the parents' notion that 'listening' is the single most important quality of a learner, we had further conversations with them. Parents stressed that children need to listen or how else would they learn? I explained and demonstrated the concept of learning through play in great depth. Sultana said: "Learning through play makes it fun doesn't it? More natural rather than a chore." Lipa contemplated on her own home learning environment: "In school, the way they teach through playing, we [speaking on behalf of the culture] don't. We teach them to sit down and learn. The school gives them something that we don't." Interestingly, this discussion suggests a shift in mindset and willingness of parents to engage with the advice of teachers.

To further support this, Special Book entries that provide snapshots of what children are learning now also include greater emphasis on the Characteristics of Effective Learning. More attention is drawn to learning through trial and error, persistence, testing ideas and problem solving. The response from parents in these Special Books has been great as they comment specifically on how their child has learnt, such as "*Wow, I like the way you kept on trying.*" I also explained during the discussion that parents should feel welcome to write in whatever language they preferred and so some have started to write in Bengali, with one noting: "*You are so brave now. I remember when you were scared of this.*" In follow-up discussions with the parents, it seems that they have grown to understand this better. I saw how willing and tolerant parents could be, for example, in allowing their children to have a go at putting on their coat and collecting their bag themselves. And even better, I overheard conversations between the parents asking one another what their child had done today. What appears to be forming is a culture of appreciation; appreciation, that is, of the child as an individual learner.

What can we learn?

I opened the chapter with a vignette on how a particular parent's viewpoint had changed from her engagement with the nursery. With English as her second language, despite being highly educated in her country of origin, she still found it tricky to tap into the British school system until her daughter began at our nursery school. Lipa was then able to interact with staff who understood her, access parent volunteering opportunities such as Forest School and engage in discussions about how she spoke about her child's early learning. Prior to that, no one had asked for her opinion, no one had bothered before – including during her son's early education in Italy. As a result, her understanding of pedagogy has developed and this has impacted her child, who has made significant progress. Formerly a selective mute, her child is now so much more confident to speak in a group. This, I would argue, is a result of interactions between the school and the home, exchanging knowledge for the betterment of the child's development and education. The case of Lipa showcases how formative assessment beyond the nursery can lead to truly positive outcomes.

Most of the quotations included in this chapter have been translated from Bengali, which is testament to why it is so important to employ bilingual staff to work with families in diverse communities. It would have also been impossible for me to have engaged with the parents in such detail had I not built relationships with them over time. This can be a problematic issue for many researchers trying to conduct studies into BME parents' views.

Although it must be remembered that I focused on a small yet representative sample group, the findings nonetheless are positive and demonstrate the value of dialogue with parents – we never quite know what they are thinking unless we talk to them, and vice versa. Whether you have a parent like Sultana who is educated in the UK and has experienced the system herself, or a parent like Tara who has been educated in a different country and then migrated, or parents like Dilwara or Zuleyka who have had very limited exposure to education, the conclusion is still the same. We must do more to listen to our parents because they have lots to say – information that is invaluable to access. They are the experts on their children; we are the experts on pedagogy. Together, we can enable children to have the best outcomes by acting immediately on what we know jointly about their interests and learning – acting on formative assessment for learning.

As a teacher, I have learnt a great deal from the discussions. First, do not be afraid to ask questions. I held my own assumptions about parents and read their unwillingness to speak about their child's learning as their undervaluing of early years. I was wrong. All of these parents care deeply about their children's individual learning trajectories, they just need both reassurance that we want to hear what they have to say and guidance from us on how they can support their young learners. Challenges that come with working in culturally diverse communities will continue – they will not be eradicated overnight, but I hope what I have demonstrated is that through speaking to parents, listening and responding to them, educators can begin to unpick and overcome such challenges. After all, this chapter clearly shows that parents are willing to engage if we show our keenness to hear them. As Askir said: *"Parents are stakeholders. Collaboration is important. So important."*

A larger scale and more in-depth study could be conducted with the aim of capturing the voices of particular ethnic groups regarding their child's early learning. The ideas discussed in this chapter require further unpicking and elaborating upon, using a similar format to Whalley's Parents Involvement in Children's Learning project or Athey's Froebel Research Project. Moreover, it would be interesting to see whether parent couples share the same expectations and ideas and how this is negotiated in the home learning environment, and how this in itself may impact interaction with the school.

I would like to conclude with a comment from a parent that really captured the school-parent relationship that we so highly value – that emphasis on coming together to support every individual child's development:

> In the beginning, I had a very bad experience with her feeding habits. So because of that reason, her key person showed me the way. Now I don't say a harsh word to my daughter. Because the way you are showing me do this, do that, she might change if you try this and you would try it too. So I did it. And the result was awesome. So without your advice . . . (shakes head) . . . I don't know what I would have done.

References

Athey, C. (1990) *Extending Thought in Young Children*. London: Paul Chapman

Athey, C. (2007) *Extending Thought in Young Children* (2nd ed.). London: Sage, p. 209.

Bronfenbrenner, U. and Condry, J. (1978) *Two Worlds of Childhood*. New York, NY: Pocket Books.

Brooker, L. (2002) *Starting School*. Buckingham: Open University Press.

Central Advisory Council for Education (1967) *Children and Their Primary Schools*. London: Her Majesty's Stationery Office.

Department for Education (2005) *Higher Standards, Better Schools for All* (Online). www.educationengland.org.uk/documents/pdfs/2005-white-paper-higher-standards.pdf (Last accessed 7 July 2017)

Department for Education (2007a) *The Children's Plan* (Online). www.gov.uk/government/uploads/system/uploads/attachment_data/file/325111/2007-childrens-plan.pdf (Last accessed 2 July 2017)

Department for Education (2007b) *Every Parent Matters* (Online). http://webarchive.nationalarchives.gov.uk/20130323054751/www.education.gov.uk/publications/eOrderingDownload/DFES-LKDA-2007.pdf (Last accessed 7 July 2017)

Department for Education (2015) *Commission on Assessment without Levels: Final Report* (Online). www.gov.uk/government/uploads/system/uploads/attachment_data/file/483058/Commission_on_Assessment_Without_Levels_-_report.pdf. (Last accessed 5 July 2017)

Early Education (2012) *Development Matters in the Early Years Foundation Stage (EYFS)* (Online). https://early-education.org.uk/development-matters (Last accessed 29 June 2017)

Hamilton, P. (2013) Fostering effective and sustainable home – school relations with migrant worker parents: A new story to tell? *International Studies in Sociology of Education*, 23 (4), 298–317 (Online). http://dx.doi.org/10.1080/09620214.2013.815439 (Last accessed 1 July 2017)

Hornby, G. (2011) *Parental Involvement in Childhood Education*. New York, NY: Springer.

Joly, D. (1984) The opinions of Mirpuri parents in Saltley, Birmingham, about their children's schooling, *Centre for the Study of Islam and Christian-Muslims Relations, Birmingham, Muslims in Europe*. Research Paper No. 23, September.

Ofsted (Office for Standards in Education) (2004) *Achievement of Bangladeshi Heritage Pupils* (Online). http://dera.ioe.ac.uk/4836/7/Achievement%20of%20 Bangladeshi%20heritage%20pupils%20%28PDF%20format%29_Redacted.pdf (Last accessed 2 July 2017)

Ogilvy, C. M., Boath, E., Cheyne, W. M., Jahoda, G. and Schaffer, H. R. (1990) Staff attitudes and perceptions in multi-cultural nursery school. *Early Child Development and Care*, 64, 1–13.

Siraj-Blatchford, I., Sylva, K., Muttock, S., Gilden, R. and Bell, D. (2002) *Researching Effective Pedagogy in the Early Years*. DfES Research Report 365. Queen's Printer. London: HMSO.

Sylva, K., Melhuish, E., Sammons, P., Siraj-Blatchford, I. and Taggart, B. (2004) *The Effective Provision of Pre-School Education (EPPE) Project: Final Report: A Longitudinal Study Funded by the DfES 1997–2004* (Online). http://eprints.ioe. ac.uk/5309/1/sylva2004EPPEfinal.pdf (Last accessed 5 July 2017)

Vygotsky, L. S. (1978) *Interaction Between Learning and Development* (M. Lopez-Morillas, Trans.). In M. Cole, V. John-Steiner, S. Scribner, and E. Souberman (eds.), *Mind in Society: The Development of Higher Psychological Processes* (pp. 79–91). Cambridge, MA: Harvard University Press.

Whalley, M. (2017) *Involving Parents in Their Children's Learning: A Knowledge-Sharing Approach* (3rd ed.). London: Sage.

Wood, D. J., Bruner, J. S. and Ross, G. (1976) The role of tutoring in problem solving. *Journal of Child Psychiatry and Psychology*, 17 (2), 89–100.

Celebrating Children's Learning outdoors

A Forest School approach

Lesley Webb

> Ahmed has climbed up in a tree. *"Look at me, I'm high up in the sky. I can go up like the birds up like the sky."* He looks down at me, *"Lesley, why is it we didn't climb trees at Forest School last week? Is it because it was stormy?"*

In 1911, Margaret McMillan opened her first open-air nursery school, and her ideas on the importance of the outdoor environment and children's health are as significant today as they were then. With the increase in obesity and concerns about physical inactivity, outdoor learning is a vital link to the health, well-being and cognitive development of young children. After a rise in childhood obesity figures over the last two decades, there had been a levelling off over the past few years. However, the figures for 2015–16 show that 9.3% of four- and five-year-olds starting school are classified as obese (the figure rises to 22% if overweight children are included). This is a rise from 9.1% the previous year. For children at the end of Reception year in the most deprived areas of the country, the obesity rate is 12.5% compared to 11.7% in the least deprived areas (NHS digital report, 2016). The Health Survey for England (HSE) 2008 and 2012 found that the proportion of boys who met the weekly physical activity guidelines (60 minutes, or more, on all seven days) fell from 28% in 2008 to 21% in 2012. For girls, the figures were 19% in 2008, falling to 16% in 2012. Research continues to demonstrate the benefits of outdoor learning: Bilton (2002), Ouvry (2003), Stephenson (2003) and White (2015), to name just a few.

In this chapter, I will argue that the well-known benefits of outdoor learning can be enhanced by the Forest School approach, but in order to assess those benefits, we cannot reduce children's experiences and outcomes to a number. Instead of simply ascribing a score to each area of learning for each child, we need to watch and listen carefully to the subtle, and yet meaningful, changes wrought by the impact of being outdoors.

For some children in the early years, most of their learning takes place outside and some things can, indeed, only be learnt outside, e.g. the feel of the wind and the rain on your face or the effort required to walk through long grass. Given this, it is obviously important for us to be observing, assessing and planning for outdoor learning.

The philosophy of Reggio Emilia envisages a 'partnership of learning' (Gandini, 1993, p. 7), where children, practitioners and the wider community become co-constructors of meaning in the learning process (Rinaldi, 1998). Municipal infant-toddler centres and preschools in this small town in Italy have pioneered an approach where all children, especially those who could be marginalized, are considered full of potential and possibilities. Among other things, the approach values active listening to children's voices, thoughts and opinions, as much as teachers'. It values the documentation of children's learning to make their thinking and theorising visible.

The 'pedagogy of listening' is a central element of the Reggio approach and is closely linked to the documentation of children's learning processes and strategies. Thus, when I observed Amina in the garden finding multiple uses for a large cardboard tube, I was excited to turn the episode into a learning story that, when shared with her key person and parents, became a document that led to a rich discussion of her as a creative thinker and enabled all to better understand Amina as a learner. This, I believe, is far more powerful than reducing learning to data.

Similarly, the Celebrating Children's Learning section of the East London Early Years and Schools Partnership website offers examples of assessments that demonstrate the Characteristics of Effective Learning. Many of these are of children learning outdoors. For example:

Alexander loves playing outdoors. He is fascinated with sand and spends extended periods of time in the large sandpit and mud kitchen. He explores the properties of sand by mixing it with water and other natural materials. Alexander makes comparisons between sand and soil, saying in his home language that we use soil to plant flowers and sand to build castles. He finally decides to make a cake by mixing both ingredients with other available resources. He remains highly engaged in his exploration.

Or

Jacob, you were playing in the sandpit, you were using a watering can to pour water down a pipe into the sand pit. You said, "*Look, I made a super flood. I need to try it from the other side.*" You found a piece of pipe. Then you poured water down the pipe and watched it flow into the second pipe. You had to readjust the position of the guttering a few times until the water flowed straight into it. Then you found a piece of guttering and added that onto the pipe and tested whether the water would flow into the guttering as well; it did and you were pleased, saying, "*Look, look.*" Next, you found a piece of pipe and put this at the end of the guttering leaning up against the edge of the sand pit. Then you poured the water down the pipe and watched it flow along the pipe, gutter and then up the pipe leaning against the side of the sand pit. We both watched it flow back down again. Then you collected some sand and put it in the guttering – I asked you what you thought might happen, you told me, "*It will block the water, maybe make another flood.*" You watched the water flowing down and saw it backing up behind the sand and flowing over. You let other children help with putting water down the pipes.

Sadly, it is still the case that, as Helen Bilton states (2002, p. 1), "Sometimes the outdoor play area is an area which is not part of the overall planning, it is not resourced or managed well, is not evaluated and is an area in which staff do not work with children." Even where the outdoor area is well resourced, it may still only be planned for in terms of 'box filling': indicating what will be put out where, but without any evaluation or showing any real value for the children's learning outside. Or, conversely, practitioners can spend all their time outside observing and writing observations and no time engaging with the children in their play. These observations may be used as part of summative assessments of the children, but they often seem to have no formative purpose as they are not used to inform the following day's or week's planning for the outdoor area. To quote Bilton (2002, p. 80), "Staff need to plan carefully, evaluate what has occurred in the day, observe what children are doing and saying and evaluate the effectiveness of the resources."

Taken from the East London Early Years and Schools Partnership website:

Kiannah, look at you climbing up the steps while holding the large wooden blocks to place onto the top of the wooden tower you and I had built. You climbed up, bending your knees when you needed to, so you could hold your balance while you were climbing with the blocks. Once you got to the top, you carefully placed the block down and then clapped, saying: "*I did it Sunni.*"

What learning did I see?

Kiannah, we all know how aware you are of your limits and how much you are capable of doing. You know when to bend down to support your balance as you found your feet.

Links to the Early Years Foundation Stage

Physical Development
Moving and handling: Handles tools, objects, construction and malleable materials safely and with increasing control

Possibilities and Opportunities

Maybe you would like to build a taller tower with your friends, taking it in turns and problem solving together.

What is interesting here is that the Possibilities and Opportunities section gives practitioners the opportunity to reflect on Kiannah's achievements and think about what they might do to extend her learning further. This sort of assessment, which is rich in detail, can then be used to inform future planning that, in turn, could include the role of the adult in supporting Kiannah to build with another child.

The Without Walls programme (Oxfordshire County Council and Learning through Landscapes, 2009) encouraged practitioners to develop their outdoor areas based on what the children were observed to be interested in and benefit from – not on what they thought would look nice, or be good for children. In the same vein, Newham Outdoors (2010), a project supporting early years practitioners to develop outdoor areas through 'listening' to children, was an action research programme aimed at developing the use of outdoor environments in schools and settings to nurture children's social and emotional development and communication skills:

> Prior to the commencement of the programme, all practitioners took part in training which focused on embedding the principles of effective observation, assessment and planning with a particular focus on engaging children and families in the process. Throughout the Spring and Summer terms 2010, three separate action research projects were developed to improve the quality of provision and practitioners' confidence in planning for personal, social and emotional development. In each project, practitioners were encouraged to identify a 'buddy' from a setting that had a similar line of enquiry. 'Buddies' were expected to visit each other on a regular basis to evaluate progress, plan next steps and problem-solve solutions.
>
> Practitioners actively consulted with children throughout the project to find out what they liked and disliked about the setting's outdoor space and how it could be improved. Children were encouraged to capture their thoughts through drawing, photographs and film.
>
> (Early Education, 2010)

We take the same approach to Forest School at Sheringham Nursery School. Once a week, we take a group of 12 children to an area of the local park for Forest School activities. This is a public park in a disadvantaged area: although the park authorities have set up a 'camp area' with logs to sit on, it is hard to let children roam freely. On Forest School days, my colleague and I visit the site first thing in the morning to clear up any rubbish. As well as the usual bottles and cans, we regularly find used needles and condoms and this, combined with the issue of dog fouling, means we can never be confident about allowing free exploration.

The Forest School philosophy originates in Scandinavia from a wish to give children an appreciation of the natural world and encourage an interest in nature conservation later in life. It was introduced in the UK following a trip by students at Bridgwater College to Denmark. They were impressed to see children freely exploring the outdoor environment, growing in confidence and learning to appreciate the natural world. The pioneering German educator Friedrich Froebel, who first created kindergarten in 1840, also placed a strong emphasis on nature:

> To make education meaningful we have to start with the environment, for it's life that educates. Our relationship with nature, with the trees and flowers and animals around us will lead to reflective thinking.
>
> (Liebschner, 1993, p. 54)

When doing our training as Forest School leaders, we had to design and carry out a series of six lesson plans. Over time, we have revised our approach so that each week we notice how a particular group of children respond and plan the following week accordingly. For instance, if they are keen on collecting sticks, flowers, leaves etc., then we will plan an activity to make a 'collecting' crown' or a 'natural mobile'.

We used to be armed with a series of plans that documented a different activity, its aims and objectives, and the role of the adult. Now, at the end of the session each week, we discuss what has gone well, what the children have shown a particular interest in and what we should do the following week. We also plan 'in the moment': returning to Ahmed up in the tree and asking why we had not done this the week before, I replied that it had indeed been Storm Doris that prevented us the previous week. This led to a discussion on the effects of the storm that we had witnessed and why it would not have been safe to climb trees. This enabled Ahmed to continue making connections in his learning, to reinforce his ideas on keeping safe and to learn about some of the more destructive forces of nature. As Eve Bearne (2017, p. 76) argues, "Formative assessment does not carry with it the implications of ranking or grading; with its dynamic elements of response and feedback, it represents more of a conversation with learners."

Shareef has been undertaking his Level 3 Forest School Leader training. As part of this, he has been taking a small group of six children to Forest School for six weeks. One of the children, Shonelle, has Down syndrome and is accompanied by Emelija, her 1:1 support worker. As part of the verification process, I go to observe Shareef's last session.

I know that he has been concerned over whether he is meeting Shonelle's needs, as we talk regularly. He has observed that if she walks to the session, then she is too tired to fully participate when she gets there. He has also noticed that if she doesn't have a snack before they go, then she will need one as soon as they get there. What I see is how skilfully he has woven these observations into a session that perfectly matches Shonelle's needs by including her in all that is going on in a differentiated fashion. So, following a quick snack, she rides to the Forest School site in our wagon (used to convey all the equipment we need), then the group splits so that Shareef takes a larger group to mark out the boundary on one side and Emelija takes Shonelle and another child to do a shorter stretch. Shonelle is able to manage the more limited walking and is also cajoled, with songs and humour, into walking most of the way back again. The whole group treats her with consideration and respect, due in large part to Shareef's positive example, and she is able to enjoy her Forest School experience and develop her gross motor skills.

To give another example of planning in the moment: a group of children were having their first session at Forest School. This involved an introduction to the use of flags to mark the boundaries. The concept and language had to be reinforced several times to ensure understanding and allow us to give the children some freedom within the boundaries. After marking out the area, we then set about making a 'bug hotel'. This required the use of saws and, inevitably, children waiting for a turn. On completing the activity, I noticed that some children were getting restless and so quickly changed the planned activity of finding a suitable place for the bug hotel to allowing the children to run freely and explore the long grass and a pile of woodchips, which proved a great place to jump. We were able to return to the bug hotel site later.

This kind of noticing, reviewing and altering plans is what good early years educators are doing all the time. We need to recognise this as assessment for learning, and ensure that we are not coerced into slavishly following a plan. In addition, when planning for children's learning outdoors, we try to provide opportunities to encounter and solve problems, increase their motivation, concentration and confidence, take charge of their own learning, follow their interests and manage some 'risky freedom' so that they become aware of their own capabilities and regulate challenge for themselves. "Children need to learn about risk – about their own capabilities and to develop the mechanisms for judging it in controlled settings" (Cook and Heseltine, 1998, p. 4). My colleague Laura Watanabe was the first to be trained in the Forest School approach and introduce it to Sheringham Nursery School. For her National Professional Qualification for Middle Leadership (NPQML), she focussed on the impact of Forest School on the children's development: "I was able to show that a more challenging outdoor environment where children are encouraged to self-risk assess and work collaboratively with one another has proven results of increased Personal, Social and Emotional and Physical Development scores" (Laura Watanabe, unpublished NPQML report, 2015).

Laura did not reduce the children's achievements and developments to mere scores. Although it was important to see the impact on their progress, it was even more important to reflect, discuss and consider the impact on children that would not necessarily show in assessment data. What about Jerome, an overweight child with special needs who speaks occasional single words? On each walk to the Forest School site, he commented on more and more things he could see: *"Cat," "Bird," "Tree"* and, as the weeks went by, started to put two words together: *"Leaves blow," "Big stick."* More than that, he spent much of his time at the site running freely around the designated area, beaming with joy. Surely, this is hugely important for his development and well-being – and it cannot be reduced to a number! Or take Dwaine, a child on the autistic spectrum who typically needs a secure routine and finds deviation from the usual pattern of the day difficult. However, he has no difficulty leaving nursery and coming with us to Forest School and loves it so much that he talks to his dad about it each week.

Being with these children and noticing the impact that being out in the natural environment has on them is a pleasure and a privilege. More than that, it has taught me that there is even more to be gained from outdoor learning than I had realised. The benefits of outdoor activity and access to nature have been well documented and researched (Morris, 2003; Travlou, 2006). However, I have seen for myself how reconnecting with nature helps children not only understand more about the world around them, but feel part of something bigger and more important, developing their independence, self-esteem and language as well as physical skills. This has further strengthened my passion for outdoor learning and Forest School in particular.

Extract from Zahid's learning story

During our fourth session of Forest School, I noticed that you were trying really hard to put on your own waterproofs. When we got to the site, you wanted to have a go at climbing a tree, making this choice for yourself. Although you found this challenging, you persevered until you managed to get to the second branch; you were so happy to have made it that you shouted to all your friends to look and gave them a beaming smile.

The next week, we made medallions and, again, you really persevered with the saw, eventually managing to cut though the wood. *"Look, I did it!"* you said proudly.

Zahid, at times it has been difficult to motivate you to do things for yourself and make choices. Over the weeks at Forest School, I noticed you becoming more and more independent. You were happy and even excited to take part in everything and showed pleasure in demonstrating your physical skills. You started to make choices and talk about your interests. I am now looking forward to seeing this impact on you in nursery too.

Parents' voice

Zahid has improved a lot since his first week at the Forest School. At first, he didn't participate but towards the end, he joined in and developed his independence.

Forest School was deemed to be such a success that when our garden at Sheringham Nursery School was redesigned, we wanted to give it much more of a natural feel and approach; we wanted to replicate and extend some of the activities that children benefited from so much. We included a fire pit, as the children are fascinated when we make a very small, contained fire in a Kelly Kettle at Forest School, as we were unable to have an open fire in the park. We have also included a tree house and two large sand areas, one with a water tap, with logs to climb and a wall to jump from. Since the garden has been altered, we have noticed a significant change in the children's engagement. This has led us to rethink our approach to bikes. Previously, many children got the bikes out every day and spent as much time as they could riding round and round on them. We noticed that this was generally a solitary activity, which did not involve any interaction or collaboration, and that there was little opportunity for children to make much progress. The child who started the year going round and round the garden on a bike would often still choose to do exactly that at the end of the year. The newly designed areas of the garden, where there are more natural features and more challenges, have engaged the children more and they have responded by sometimes choosing to play and overcome challenges on their own, and sometimes interacting with others – for example, using the pump to mix water and sand. We have introduced a challenging bike session, using two-wheeled bikes, in the larger playground of the primary school over the road, and seen children developing their balance and confidence greatly in those sessions. For those children – particularly boys – who arrive with limited oral language skills, solitary bike play was of limited value. Observing the children at Forest School, or engaged in similar open-ended activities in the nursery garden, we notice how much more interaction there is between them now.

A project in Wales, investigating children perceived to be underachieving, engaging in child-initiated learning outdoors concluded that:

> The more natural outdoor spaces in which child-initiated activity took place appeared, both directly (for example through provision of space and the encouragement of activities involving gross motor skills) and indirectly (e.g. through its location outside the classroom and association with fun and play) to support and amplify the effects of child initiated learning and to diminish (the perception of) underachievement.
>
> (Maynard, Waters and Clement, 2013, p. 223)

In other words, children could not only develop and learn better with access to natural outdoor spaces, but practitioners' perceptions of them as underachievers were altered.

Seeing children excel at Forest School activities continues to surprise me. It often changes and extends *my* perception of them as learners.

Anton was a shy boy. An only child but with a sibling on the way, he took a long time to settle. Once settled, he made friends with two girls and played mostly with them. He was still easily upset. He played both inside and outside but never appeared to really challenge himself physically.

> During his Forest School sessions, he proved to be an outstanding tree climber. He was confident and capable, going higher than anyone else. He would make sure to test the branches to see if they would take his weight and, if one route was no good, he would change strategy to try another.

Our school is set in a densely populated, disadvantaged area of East London. Many parents are reluctant to access the local park due to a fear of dogs or 'undesirables'. This makes the need for access to high-quality outdoor learning and space to move, run, climb and jump imperative. It also highlights the need to include parents. The Early Years Foundation Stage (EYFS) framework reinforces the importance of the outdoors and the necessity of working in partnership with parents. As Gortmaker et al. (1999) argue (quoted in Hughes and Fleming, 2013, pp. 279–291):

> Building on the key socialising role of parents in cultivating amongst their children positive attitudes towards engagement in physical activity (NICE, 2007), an important consideration is the competence and confidence of parents in supporting their children's learning in physical development, and paradoxically it is often physical skills that require most practice.

In addition, tackling childhood obesity has become a major public health imperative (Department of Health, 2012). For the first time, the report of the Chief Medical Officers (2011) included the specific recommendation that children under five, as soon as they are able to walk, need to be active for three hours a day. This highlights the need to work closely with parents to encourage them to recognise the relevance and importance of physical activity on their child's overall well-being and development. Returning to my original point about the inadequacy of reducing such development to a number, how much more meaningful it is to say to a parent, *"Your child had a really successful first time at Forest School this week; they managed to put on their own waterproofs and while we were there, they explored the site freely, discovering toadstools, mini-beasts, flowers and cherries"* rather than *"Oh yes, they are at 40–60 months for Health and Self-Care and 30–50 for Understanding the World."*

Quantitative data is important for us as a school. We need to be able to assess children's progress, demonstrate that we are doing a good job and ensure that we provide good value for money. But parents want to know that their child had a good time, that they managed a new experience successfully and that they learnt something from it. As a teacher, I also need to ensure that I build on those meaningful experiences, using formative assessment, discussing with parents, noticing and analysing to build further on the child's learning. In addition, it is incumbent upon us to point out that time spent learning outdoors or in Forest School is also contributing significantly to the child's three hours of physical activity for that day and hence their health and well-being.

As part of our aim not only to get, but also to keep, parents on board with our Forest School programme, we have adapted the National Trust's '50 things to do before you are 11 ¾' booklet to a leaflet titled '20 things to do before you are 5'. Some of these things, such as climb a tree or hunt for mini-beasts, we will do at Forest School and we ask the parents to continue to try and achieve the rest in their own time. The leaflet is introduced at a short parents' meeting held for each new group of Forest Schoolers where we also describe the importance of what we are doing. In Chapter 4 of this book, Tania Choudhury describes how this has had a particular impact on many Bengali parents, who mention Forest School as having a profound impact on their children. Additionally, listening to parents' feedback on what their child has told them about Forest School, how they have taken on board the activities as a family or how they have applied the learning in other situations all contributes to building a rounded picture of that child, enabling our assessments to be more accurate.

Parent of Maurice:

"He used to stamp on spiders, now he says to me, 'Mummy, you mustn't kill it!' "

In conclusion, outdoor learning in general, and Forest School in particular, can have a profound effect on children's learning, development and well-being. This may not always be reflected as data, and I have argued that it does not need to be. What is important is that we observe and listen to children. We need to notice what the impact is, notice their interests and consider what we need to do to help them develop further. Sometimes, we need to respond to children immediately, and other times, we need to plan for the next day or the following week. But it is this cycle of respectful observation, dialogue, planning and reviewing children's learning outdoors that has enabled us to find our own way of working towards what the Reggio Emilia preschools aspire to: children, practitioners and the wider community learning together and becoming co-constructors of meaning.

References

Bearne, E. (2017) Assessing children's written text: A framework for equity. *Assessment, Accountability and Policy UKLA*, 51 (2), 74–83.
Bilton, H. (2002) *Outdoor in the Early Years Management and Innovation* (2nd ed.). London: David Fulton Publishers.

Chief Medical Officers (2011) *New Physical Activities Guidelines* (Online). www.gov.uk/government/news/new-physical-activity-guidelines (Last accessed 19 June 2017)

Cook, B. and Heseltine, P. J. (1998) *Assessing Risk on Children's Playgrounds* (2nd ed.). Birmingham: ROSPA.

Department of Health (2012) *2010 to 2015 Government Policy: Obesity and Healthy Eating* (Online). www.gov.uk/government/publications/2010-to-2015-government-policy-obesity-and-healthy-eating/2010-to-2015-government-policy-obesity-and-healthy-eating (Last accessed 19 June 2017)

Early Education (2010) *Newham Outdoors* (Online). www.early-education.org.uk/newham-outdoors (Last accessed 19 June 2017)

Gandini, L. (1993) Fundamentals of the Reggio Emilia approach to early childhood education. *Young Children*, 49 (1), 4–8.

Hughes, H. and Fleming, S. (2013) Play to learn: A case study of parent/carer and child engagement with a physical activity. *Education 3–13 International Journal of Primary, Elementary and Early Years Education*, 43 (3), 279–291.

Liebschner, J. (1993) The curriculum of Friedrich Froebel. *Early Years*, 14 (1), 54.

Maynard, T., Waters, J. and Clement, J. (2013) Child initiated learning, the outdoor environment and the underachieving child. *Early Years: An International Research Journal*, 33 (3), 212–225.

Morris, N. (2003) *Health Well Being and Open Space. A Literature Review*. OPEN Space Research Centre.

National Trust (2017) *50 things to do before you are 11 ¾*. www.nationaltrust.org.uk/features/50-things-to-do-before-youre-11-activity-list (Last accessed 19 June 2017)

NHS. (2008 and 2012) *The Health Survey for England (HSE)*. London: The Information Centre.

NHS. Digital report. *Child Obesity Rising Again, NHS Report Reveals* (Online). www.theguardian.com/society/2016/nov/03/child-obesity-rising-again-nhs-report-reveals (Last accessed 19 June 2017)

Ouvry, M. (2003) *Developing Muscles and Minds*. London: National Children's Bureau.

Rinaldi, C. (1998) *The Hundred Languages of Children: The Reggio Emilia Approach Advanced Reflections* (2nd ed.). Westport, CT and London: Ablex Publishing.

Sargeant, J. (2009) *Without Walls: Creative Work With Families, Developing the Outdoor Space – A Resource for Children's Centre Managers and Staff*. Oxfordshire, UK: Oxfordshire County Council.

Stephenson, A. (2003) Physical risk-taking: Dangerous or endangered? *Early Years*, 23, 35–43.

Travlou, P. (2006) *Wild Adventure Space: A Literature Review*. Edinburgh, UK: OPEN Space Research Centre.

White, J. (2015) Every Child a Mover: A Practical Guide to Providing Young Children with the Physical Opportunities They Need. Watford, UK: Early Education

Index